PLAY GUITAR
IN 10 EASY LESSONS

D1118547

PLAY GUITAR
IN 10 EASY LESSONS

A SIMPLE, BEGINNER'S GUIDE TO LEARNING GUITAR

JON BUCK

hamlyn

An Hachette UK Company
www.hachette.co.uk

First published in Great Britain in 2006 by Hamlyn, a division of Octopus Publishing Group Ltd,
Carmelite House, 50 Victoria Embankment, London EC4Y 0DZ
www.octopusbooks.co.uk
www.octopusbooksusa.com

Copyright © Octopus Publishing Group Ltd 2006, 2011, 2014, 2017
This edition first published in the U.S. in 2017

Distributed in the U.S. by Hachette Book Group, 1290 Avenue of the Americas, 4th and 5th
Floors, New York, NY 10104

Distributed in Canada by Canadian Manda Group, 664 Annette Street, Toronto, Ontario,
Canada M6S 2C8

All rights reserved. No part of this work may be reproduced or utilized in any form or by any
means, electronic or mechanical, including photocopying, recording or by any information
storage and retrieval system, without the prior written permission of the publisher.
Jon Buck asserts the moral right to be identified as the author of this work.

ISBN: 978-0-600-63504-8

A CIP catalogue record for this book is available from the British Library

Printed and bound in China

10 9 8 7 6 5 4 3 2 1

All instructions are given for a right-handed player.

Thanks to the team at Sound Control, Oxford Street, for their kind loan of equipment.

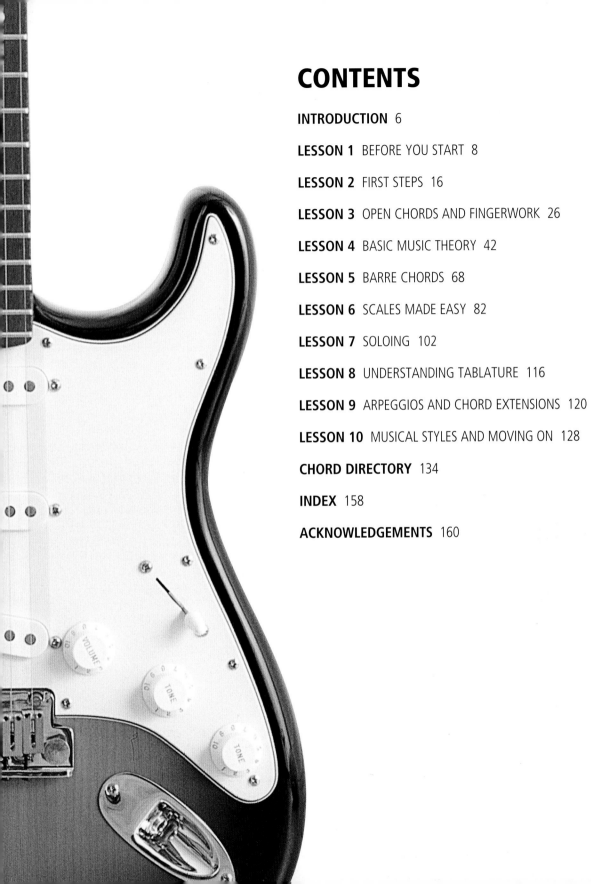

CONTENTS

INTRODUCTION

The guitar is one of the most popular and versatile instruments there is. It can be used to accompany a singer or to provide backing chords for other musicians; it is equally at home as a solo instrument or as the lead instrument in a group or ensemble. One of the most appealing things about the guitar is its ability to work within a wide and diverse range of musical styles. Everything from classical fugues to heavy metal solos can be played successfully on a guitar.

ALL YOU NEED TO KNOW

In this book you will find everything you need to know to become a competent and confident guitarist. Ten easy lessons cover everything from choosing and buying your first guitar to understanding the complexities of note relativity and improvisation. With practice you will be playing chords and solos, and using all types of techniques and tricks. You will also understand how to read tablature and how the guitar can be used to work out key signatures in standard music notation.

USING THE BOOK

There are two ways to use this book. The first is as a tuition manual. As you follow each lesson you progressively learn more about how to play the guitar, starting with basic chords, moving through barre chords and on to soloing and improvisation. You also learn the art of building chords and arpeggios (spread-out chords), so there is never a chord you cannot find.

The second way to use this book is as a reference manual. It is packed with information useful for beginners and advanced players alike. For example, many guitarists learn songs from Internet sites, where most guitar music is noted in tablature form. Lesson 8 (see pages 116–19) reveals all the main symbols and signs that can be perplexing to a guitarist. The basic music theory covered in Lesson 4 (see pages 42–67) will also be useful to guitarists of all standards: understanding written music is vital because this is the universal way in which players communicate musical ideas to other musicians. You will also find in the book many scales, modes (groups of notes that belong together), arpeggios and even a chord directory offering 382 useful chords to dip into over and over again. There are also jargon-busting explanations of technical terms throughout the lessons (look for words in italic).

PRACTISE, PRACTISE, PRACTISE

However you intend to use this book, it is essential to remember that there is no substitute for practice. No guitar tuition book can succeed in teaching you to play if you don't put in the work with the instrument on your knee. Practise every day and you will soon be playing your favourite songs and solos – and maybe even writing songs and solos of your own. Good luck!

LESSON 1 BEFORE YOU START

AIM TO CHOOSE AND PURCHASE AN INSTRUMENT THAT SUITS ALL YOUR REQUIREMENTS, TO BE ABLE TO NAME ALL ITS PARTS AND TO KNOW HOW TO TUNE AND RESTRING IT.

Choosing the right guitar is vital: instruments can be expensive and if you get one that doesn't suit you it can make learning the basics much harder. Here's how to get it right.

CHOOSING and BUYING a guitar

Get to know the three main types of guitar outlined here before you consider buying one: you need to make sure the instrument you choose suits your needs before getting out your wallet. Consider second-hand guitars, which often offer better value for money than new models, but take advice from someone familiar with guitars, who can help you choose one worth having. Buy the best you can afford: a poor quality instrument makes playing harder.

CLASSICAL ACOUSTIC GUITAR

◀ Most beginners choose this type of guitar because it is relatively cheap. These guitars originate from Spain and tend to have wide, flat fingerboards that may cause problems if you have small hands. The strings are made of nylon, which reduces the amount of tension on the neck; this means there is no *truss rod*.

STEEL STRING ACOUSTIC GUITAR

ELECTRIC GUITAR

▲ These guitars usually have a bigger body than the classical acoustic and the fingerboard tends to be thinner and slightly curved for ease of playing, especially if you have small hands. Because the strings are made of steel and so the tension is higher than for nylon strings, the narrow neck has a strengthening rod within, allowing you to adjust the *action* to make playing easier.

▲ Very easy to play, this type of guitar is extremely popular. It plugs into an amplifier to increase volume. The neck and fingerboard tend to be thin and slightly curved for easy playing. Remember that you will need to buy an amplifier, an extra expense.

JARGON BUSTER

Truss rod Metal tensioning rod that runs up the inside of the neck on a steel string guitar and can be adjusted to keep the neck straight.

Action Distance between the fingerboard (see annotated guitars, pages 10–11) and the strings.

ANATOMY of the guitar

Familiarize yourself with the various parts of a guitar and you'll have a better understanding of what to look for when trying out different models before buying. There are big differences in the design of acoustic and electric instruments, all described in the glossary of guitar parts below. Make sure you feel comfortable with all these terms before moving on with the lesson.

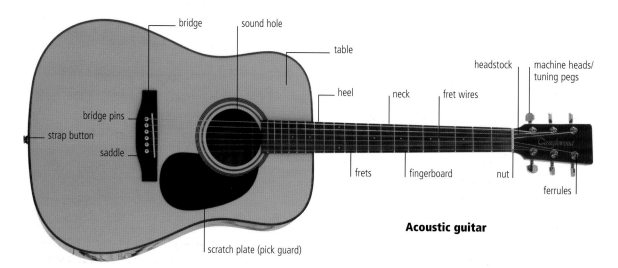

Acoustic guitar

GLOSSARY OF ACOUSTIC GUITAR TERMS

Table Top, or front, of the main body of the guitar. On better quality guitars this part is made of solid wood, but most commonly it is laminate (pieces of wood glued together).
Sound hole Generates sound from the vibration of strings.
Bridge Holds the strings in place on the table.
Saddle Where the vibrating section of string starts at the bridge end. Usually made of plastic or brass.
Bridge pins Hold the strings in place at the bridge.
Scratch plate Prevents plectrum scratching the guitar body.
Heel Support at the back of the neck that holds the body and neck firmly together.
Strap button Where the strap attaches to the guitar, usually at the base of the body and on the heel.
Neck Usually made from two pieces of wood: one forms the back, the other the fingerboard.

Truss rod On steel string acoustic guitars this metal tensioning rod runs up the inside of the neck and can be adjusted to keep the neck straight.
Fingerboard Composed of fret wires and frets; it is usually made from rosewood, but may be a cheaper alternative.
Fret wires Wires hammered into the fingerboard to divide it into intervals of a semitone.
Frets Gaps in which to place your fingers to create notes.
Nut Slotted piece of plastic or brass through which strings run. It keeps the strings in place and is where the vibrating section of string ends.
Headstock This houses the ferrules and machine heads.
Machine heads/tuning pegs Turn these to tune the guitar.
Ferrules These are the part of the machine head to which the strings attach.

bridge   saddles   pick-ups   body   strap button

headstock   machine heads/ tuning pegs

neck   fret wires

frets   fingerboard   nut

ferrules

scratch plate (pick guard)

Electric guitar

pick-up selector switch

jack socket

volume/ tone controls

GLOSSARY OF ELECTRIC GUITAR TERMS

Body Usually made of two or three pieces of wood glued together. Some better guitars have one-piece bodies.

Scratch plate Made of plastic; hides the wiring for pick-ups and control knobs.

Bridge Adjustable saddles housed here hold the strings in place at the body end of the guitar.

Saddles Each string runs over a saddle at the body end, where the vibrating section of string starts. They can be adjusted for height and length.

Tremolo arm Used to increase or decrease tension on the strings. It moves the bridge to give a wavering note effect.

Pick-ups Magnetically pick up the vibration of the strings and amplify the sound.

Volume control Adjusts the loudness of the guitar through the amplifier.

Tone controls Adjust the bass and treble sound of the guitar through the amplifier.

Pick-up selector switch Chooses which pick-up is working and therefore changes the sound of the guitar through the amplifier.

Jack socket Where the lead plugs in from the amplifier.

Strap button Where the strap attaches to the guitar.

WHAT TO CHECK BEFORE BUYING

1 Make sure machine heads turn freely.

2 Look down the length of the neck from the headstock end, checking that the neck isn't twisted. A slight curve is fine (the truss rod is there to sort that out), but a twisted neck is a problem and should be avoided.

3 Plug an electric guitar into an amplifier and pick through each string, slowly checking that the volume of each is similar. Difference in the volume of strings can indicate faulty pick-ups.

4 With an electric guitar, stand in front of the amplifier with the volume up. Don't play, just listen to see if you can hear any feedback. If you can, the pickups aren't isolated properly and need replacing. Don't buy a guitar with this problem.

5 Listen to an electric guitar through the amplifier alone, without using effects equipment. Effects units can make a bad guitar sound great because they enhance the sound produced.

▼ View straight down the neck from the headstock.

TUNING and RESTRINGING

A guitar sounds dreadful when out of tune, so it's important in your first lesson to learn how to successfully tune your instrument (there are three methods to choose from). You should check and adjust your tuning every time you start a practice session. When you first break a string you will want to know how to restring your guitar. Step-by-step instructions follow.

STRING NAMES

Most guitars have six strings. Remember the order and names of these strings by memorizing the phrase **E**very **A**pple **D**oes **G**et **B**etter **E**veryday: the first letter of each word gives you the name of the string, from the 6th and lowest string at the top of the diagram to the 1st and highest string at the bottom of the diagram.

					E 6th string
					A 5th string
					D 4th string
					G 3rd string
					B 2nd string
					E 1st string

TUNING A GUITAR

There are three main methods of tuning guitar strings. Experiment until you find the one you feel most comfortable with. Electronic tuners are very cheap and offer a failsafe way of ensuring that your guitar is always in tune to perfect, or concert, pitch. This allows you to play along, in tune, with other musicians and with recordings. Other products like tuning forks and pitch pipes are not as accurate.

▲ A standard guitar tuner. Notice the digital needle on the screen and the lights just above it.

Using a tuner

1 Set the tuner to E. While it is ringing, pick (pluck) the 1st string on the guitar. Make sure the string is open (you are not pressing it down on to the frets). Either a needle or a series of lights will spring into life on the tuner.

2 The aim is to tune the string so that the needle on the tuner is vertical, or the middle (usually green) light comes on. Adjust the machine head until the needle points to the 'in tune' mark or the green light only is illuminated.

3 Repeat for each of the other strings.

▲ Make sure that your finger is clear of the string below it, so that you can play both strings together, to check the tuning.

TOP TIP

The horizontal lines of the fingerboard diagrams on this page represent the six strings on the guitar (see diagram, left). The vertical lines show the fret wires, with a double line representing the nut where the fingerboard meets the headstock. The position of the fingers is indicated by round dots. A string played open (without any fingers on it) is marked by a circle at the nut end of the diagram. Strings that aren't picked or sounded are marked at the nut end by an X.

5th fret method

1 Play the note E on a piano or keyboard. Pick the open low E (6th) string and turn the machine head for that string clockwise or anticlockwise until the pitches are identical.

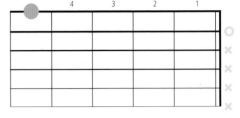

2 Place your finger on the 5th fret on the E (6th) string. Pick the string with your other hand. Then pick the open A (5th) string (the next string along). They should sound the same. If they don't, adjust the machine head for the A string.

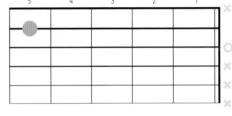

3 Place your finger on the 5th fret on the A string. Pick this string, then the next one along, the D (4th) string. Adjust the machine head, if necessary, until both strings sound the same.

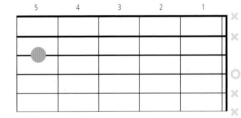

4 Repeat, with your finger on the 5th fret of the D string to tune the open G string (the 3rd string).

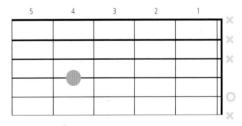

5 Move your finger to the 4th fret of the G string and compare the sound of this string when struck to that of the open B (2nd) string. Adjust the open string with the machine head if necessary.

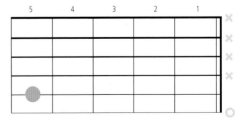

6 Move your finger to the 5th fret of the B string. Compare it to the high E (1st) string. Adjust the top string if needed.

Tuning using harmonics

1 Place any finger lightly on the A (5th) string, directly above the 12th fret wire. Pluck the string with the other hand to hear a sound known as a harmonic.

2 Place a finger over the 5th fret of the E (6th) string. Pluck the string to hear the harmonic. Repeat at the 7th fret on the A string and compare the two harmonics. Adjust the machine head of the A string until they sound exactly the same.

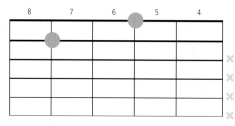

3 In the same way, sound the harmonics on the 5th fret of the A string and the 7th fret of the D (4th) string. Adjust the D string until they sound the same as one another.

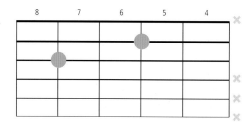

4 Sound the harmonics on the 5th fret of the D string and the 7th fret of the G (3rd) string. Adjust the G string until they sound identical.

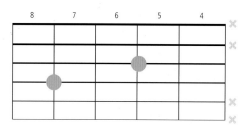

5 Play the open B (2nd) string. Sound the harmonic at the 7th fret of the low E (6th) string. Adjust the open B string until they emulate each other.

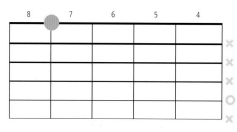

6 Play the open high E (1st) string. Sound the harmonic at the 7th fret of the A (5th) string. Adjust the open E string until they sound the same.

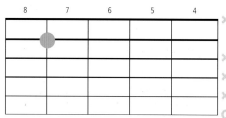

RESTRINGING A GUITAR

There are many different ways of restringing a guitar. As all guitars vary it is impossible to give advice to suit all models, but these basic guidelines should help.

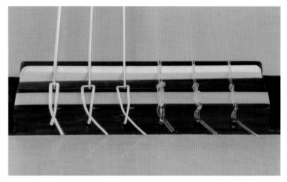

1 Always begin at the bridge (see pages 10–11). For electric and steel string guitars take the correct new string and thread the plain end through the appropriate fixture in the bridge. Pull through until the 'ball' end (the tiny metal disc) wedges tight. In some guitars the end of the string might be held in position with a vertical bridge pin.

3 Tie a nylon or classical acoustic string in place at the bridge. To see how this is done on your model look at how the other strings are tied in and try to replicate.

2 Run the string up the neck to the ferrule. Cut off electric and steel strings about 6–8 cm (2½–3½ in) past the ferrule. Bend a 1 cm (½ in) right angle in the end of the string and pass the end through the hole in the appropriate ferrule, so that only 0.5 cm (¼ in) is showing. Make sure all the strings face outward from the centre of the headstock.

4 Pass the end of a nylon or classical string through the hole in the ferrule, from front to back, then twist it back beneath itself to secure in place. Keep the loose part of the string tight in your fingers as you turn the machine head. Tune the new string using the method that you favour.

LESSON SUMMARY

By now you should have targeted which type of guitar suits your needs and have a working knowledge of its components. You have experimented with three methods of tuning and know how to change broken strings.

LESSON 2 FIRST STEPS

AIM TO UNDERSTAND HOW THE LESSONS ARE TAUGHT, TO INTRODUCE LEFT- AND RIGHT-HAND TECHNIQUES AND THE IMPORTANCE OF GOOD POSTURE AND COORDINATION.

Before you start learning to play the guitar it is important that you understand the tuition methods used in the book. All are explained in this chapter. We move on to look at basic techniques for the left and right hands, good posture and coordination.

METHODS used in the book

There are many different tuition methods used throughout the lessons, which will be explained as we progress. At this stage you just need to understand the two most common techniques – and commit them to memory before you move on, since they are used in every lesson. If you're still having problems with the terminology, go back to Lesson 1 and revise the anatomy of the guitar (see pages 10–11).

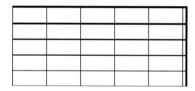

FINGERBOARD DIAGRAMS

◁ This very basic diagram of the fingerboard displays everything you need to know to be able to play its content. The horizontal lines represent the six strings on the guitar, with the low E (6th) string at the top and the high E (1st) string at the bottom. The vertical lines show the fret wires, with a double line representing the nut where the fingerboard meets the headstock.

▶ **Where to put your fingers**
The position of the fingers is indicated by round dots which are numbered and colour-coded. A string played open (without any fingers on it) is marked by a circle at the nut end of the diagram. Strings that aren't picked or sounded are marked at the nut end by an X.

Colour-coding
Blue 1st finger (index finger)
Green 2nd finger (middle finger)
Red 3rd finger (ring finger)
Yellow 4th finger (little finger)

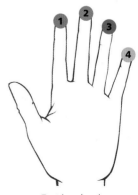

○ string played open
✕ string not played

▶ Example 1 – Chords

Chord diagrams clearly show where each finger should be placed on the fingerboard in order to play a given chord. The diagram on the right illustrates the chord C7.

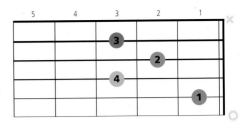

▶ Example 2 – Barred notes

When you need to play a *barre*, by laying a finger of your left hand over more than one string at a time, a solid colour-coded line joins the two outside notes that your fingers should cover.

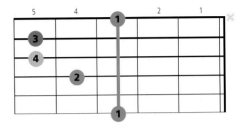

▶ Example 3 – *Scales*

This type of diagram outlines the note pattern for a scale (or consecutive run of notes). Play the notes from lowest to highest (from the 6th string to the 1st, working away from the nut on each string) and back again (from the 1st string to the 6th, working away from the bridge) playing the top note only once.

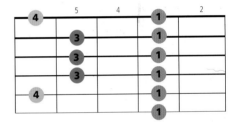

JARGON BUSTER

Barre The art of laying a left-hand finger across more than one string at a time.

Scales Patterns of notes played individually in a set order. The order is determined by the type of scale.

PHOTOGRAPHS

▶ Photos show exactly what to do with your left hand. If you read the fingerboard diagrams correctly, your hand will look like the photo, so this is a great way of double-checking that you are getting along well. The photo on the right shows the finger pattern set out in Example 1 for the C7 chord. The first finger is in the 1st fret, the second finger is in the 2nd fret and the third and fourth fingers are in the 3rd fret.

LEFT-HAND technique

The left hand presses the strings down on to the frets to create certain notes. Guitarists look for a clean sound without any buzzing from other frets and the only way to achieve this is to establish correct hand positioning. The following easy pointers will help you do that.

THUMB POSITIONS

Choose from two recognized techniques for positioning the thumb. Try both out: each has its advantages, so use whichever suits you best, and don't be afraid to mix and match if that's what feels right. It is important that you are comfortable.

▲ **Classical technique**
Press the ball of the thumb firmly against the back of the neck at all times, forming a vice-like grip around the neck. Try it now.

▲ **Alternative technique**
Many players like to move the thumb around at the back of the neck, sometimes wrapping it over the top of the fingerboard. If you have a wide fingerspan you might be able to hold the 6th or even 5th strings with your thumb. This frees all four fingers to fret other notes. Try this technique now to check whether your fingerspan is wide enough.

TOP TIP

Keep your nails short; it's impossible to fret notes if your nails are too long.

FRETTING NOTES

Practise fretting notes by pressing the tip of your finger immediately behind the fret wire. If it's too near the fret wire, the note can sound muted. If it's too far back from the fret wire the string can buzz against it. Keep your fingers vertical to the fret wire and let unused fingers hover over the strings, near enough to be ready to play, but not so near as to mute or play other strings accidentally. Have a go now at playing some random notes with different fingers.

FINGER POSITION

◀ **Correct positioning**
The tip of the finger is just behind the fret wire. Fingers are vertical to the wire. Always use the tip of the finger instead of the pad to ensure the note is crisp and clear.

◀ **Too far forward**
Here the finger is too far forward and at an angle causing the sound to be muted. There's also the risk of reverberation off a fret further forward.

◀ **Too far back**
If your finger is too far away from the intended fret wire the note will buzz against it and sound hollow.

▲ **Easy exercise**
Practise assigning one finger to a fret. Place your first finger in fret 3. Position your second finger over the 4th fret, your third finger over the 5th fret and your little finger over the 6th fret. Pick each string in turn, lifting and pressing your fingers down without altering their position.

USING THE LITTLE FINGER

You must use your little finger! Each finger provides 25 per cent of your playing potential. If you don't use your little finger, you will only ever play at 75 per cent of your potential, which impedes progress. Take your focus to your little finger often and it will increase in dexterity and strength.

DON'T PUSH IT

When you work on left-hand technique, you use muscles in your wrist and hand that seldom see action, so it is vital to stop if your hand hurts. Repetitive Strain Injury (RSI) is a common problem for guitarists who refuse to take a break. Whenever you feel your hand aching, take time out. Don't be dismayed: fingertips toughen as you practise, which makes them more durable and eventually makes playing less painful.

CHECKLIST

Thumb Choose from either the classical or alternative techniques shown opposite.

Finger angle Fingers should be vertical to the angle of the wires on the fingerboard.

Finger position The tip of the finger is positioned just behind the fret wire.

RIGHT-HAND technique

Your right hand is as important as your left hand, since it produces sound from the strings by either picking or *strumming* them. A good right-hand technique is essential for smooth, fluent playing. There are three key techniques to master and a fourth you might like to try favoured by country and folk guitarists. Whichever technique you prefer, your main aim should be the clarity that comes when you feel entirely comfortable. This is only achieved with practice.

USING A PLECTRUM

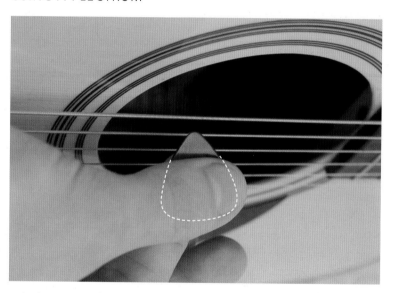

▲ A *plectrum*, or pick, is a triangular piece of plastic used for strumming strings and picking out melody lines. It gives a slightly brighter sound than fingers, and helps your sound cut through better when playing with other instruments. It is not so good for picking two or more non-adjacent strings at the same time. Hold the plectrum between your index finger and thumb, with the tip protruding about 0.5 cm (¼ in). Don't grip too tightly or too loosely. A tight grip can bring on muscle fatigue; with a loose grip the plectrum flaps around, increasing your risk of dropping it. To play with a plectrum alternate between down and up strokes. Try some up and down strokes now.

FINGER STYLE

▲ This is the art of playing with thumb and fingers. It has a much warmer sound than a plectrum, which makes it ideal for soft picking, and you can play two or more non-adjacent strings at the same time. However, finger style is not so good for soloing: it doesn't have the attack of a plectrum and can hinder the fluency of fast runs. Try out the style now by using your thumb to pick bass notes (the lower strings) while the fingers either strum or pick the treble (higher) strings.

HYBRID TECHNIQUE

▲ By far the most versatile technique, in this method you place the plectrum between index finger and thumb as in method 1, far left, and use the remaining fingers of the right hand to pick out other notes. This combination permits speed and fluency when soloing and also the ability to pick multiple strings at the same time. Try it now. Strum the strings with the plectrum between first finger and thumb; practise picking other strings with your remaining fingers.

THUMB-PICK TECHNIQUE

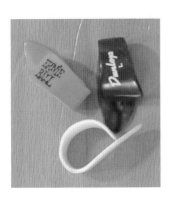

◄ Many country and folk guitarists use what is known as a 'thumb pick', a plastic device similar to a plectrum that wraps around the thumb, freeing up the index finger. The main advantage is that you have the ability to play as if using a plectrum when strumming and soloing, but keep all four fingers free to finger-pick chords.

WHAT THICKNESS OF PLECTRUM?

Plectrum thickness is an individual preference. Many players favour a thin plectrum for strumming – it offers little resistance when stroking up and down – but a thick plectrum for soloing. The resistance a thick plectrum offers means it doesn't bend, making it easier to move quickly to the next note. The important thing is that you practise enough to ensure that your choice of plectrum doesn't hinder your progress.

JARGON BUSTER

Strumming The art of stroking the strings up or down with the right hand to sound out chords.

Plectrum Also known as a pick, this is usually a triangular piece of plastic made for strumming and picking strings.

POSTURE and COORDINATION

There are two main ways to hold the guitar, either sitting or standing. Using the wrong position will affect your ability to play and can influence the coordination of your right and left hands. Here we work to establish good posture from the start, experimenting with what feels good for you.

SITTING WITH THE GUITAR

If you choose to sit, you need to decide whether to use the standard sitting position or the classical sitting position. The first is more common. You will need a firm chair without arms, or a stool, and both feet should reach flat to the floor.

▶ **Standard sitting position**

Rest the waist of the guitar – the place where it curves in at the bottom of the body – on your right thigh. Hold the instrument so the neck is relatively horizontal. Practise using a plectrum, picking a few strings to see how the position suits you. Revise the left-hand techniques (see pages 18–19). Try not to slouch as you practise, and relax your shoulders away from your ears.

▶ **Classical sitting position**

Place the waist of the guitar between your legs so it rests on your left thigh. Elevate the neck at an angle of approximately 45 degrees. You might like to use a foot stool for the foot beneath the neck. Practise the left-hand easy exercises on pages 18–19, and revise using a plectrum and finger picking in this position (see pages 20–21) to see how it suits you. If it feels comfortable, it's probably right.

STANDING WITH THE GUITAR

If you choose to stand with the guitar you will need a shoulder strap. Attach the ends of the strap to the two strap buttons, adjusting until the instrument hangs comfortably around your left shoulder. You must be able to move both hands freely, without straining your wrists. Waist height is usually best, with the neck angled slightly upward. Hanging the instrument really low on the strap, rock style, hinders your ability to fret notes correctly, increasing the chance of bum notes.

TOP TIP

Think about what you wear when playing guitar. Baggy sleeves on shirts and jumpers can catch on the strings and muffle the sound.

COORDINATION

It is important that right and left hands work well together: when you pluck a string with your right hand it has to be the one your left hand is fretting – but coordinating them takes a long time to master. Here are some exercises to practise every day that will help. They are also excellent warm-up exercises, so when you have mastered the coordination element, keep practising them anyway. They are a good way to start each daily practice session.

▶ **Exercise 1 –**

Two *octave* E *chromatic* scale

This is a great exercise to warm up with because it gets all the fingers working in the left hand, and in the right hand gives you the opportunity to work on picking technique with your plectrum or fingers. Practise three times through. Keep the left hand the same each time, fretting the notes shown one after the other, moving from the lowest string up and from the nut end toward the bridge and down again. Start by playing *open strings*. With the right hand first use all down strokes with a plectrum or your thumb only. On the second run use all up strokes with the plectrum or first finger only. Finally, alternate down and up strokes or alternate thumb and first finger.

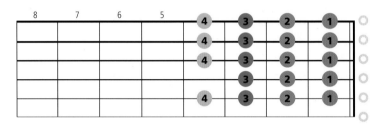

▶ **Exercise 2 –**

Two octave G chromatic scale

When you can play the first exercise fluently, move on to this one. You will notice that both scales use many open strings. Again practise three times up and down. In the first run use all down strokes with the plectrum or right thumb. The second time use all up strokes with the plectrum or first finger. Lastly use down and up strokes – alternate the thumb and first finger of your right hand.

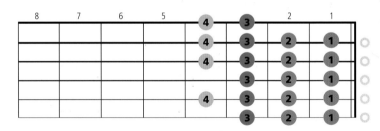

▶ Exercise 3 –
Two octave A chromatic scale

This scale has no open strings: each note is fretted, so make sure you feel comfortable with exercises 1 and 2 before moving on. Start slowly, don't try to speed up too soon. Make sure you can play all the notes correctly and clearly before attempting to increase speed. As before, practise in groups of three. The left hand is the same each time; use all down strokes in the right hand in the first run through, all up strokes in the second. In the third alternate down and up strokes or alternate thumb and first finger. Start with your first finger at the 5th fret.

JARGON BUSTER

Octave Difference in pitch between two notes of the same name.

Chromatic The word chromatic basically means 'every note', so in chromatic scales you play every note on the fingerboard within that group of sounds.

Open strings Strings played without a left-hand finger fretting a note on them.

LESSON SUMMARY

You can now understand the fingerboard diagram system used in the book and have committed the finger colour-coding and numbers to memory for instant recognition. You have experimented with sitting and standing postures to see which suits you. You have mastered left-hand finger basics and tried out key right-hand styles. And you know through the first scale exercises that mastery of control and coordination only comes with lots of practice. If you still feel unsure of anything, revise that element of the lesson and don't move on until you feel happy that you understand.

LESSON 3 OPEN CHORDS AND FINGERWORK

AIM TO BE ABLE TO PLAY ALL THE BASIC CHORDS IN THE FIVE MAIN GROUPS AND CHANGE BETWEEN THEM FLUENTLY, WHILE STRUMMING OR PICKING WITH THE RIGHT HAND.

Whatever style of music you are interested in playing on guitar, open chords should be your first area of study. Chords are formed by pressing the fingers of the left hand on to specific points on the fingerboard, while the right hand strums or picks the notes.

Basic MAJOR CHORDS

Chords are groups of notes played together. Major chords, defined by their very happy sound, are the first of five groups of chords we will study, and at this stage we will take a look at seven chords in each group. Chords in this section are divided into groups to show you their level of difficulty. It's best to learn the easy chords before the intermediate chords. As ever, the more you practise, the easier the chords will become.

EASY MAJOR CHORDS TO PRACTISE

◀ A major
Place your left-hand fingers on the fingerboard as shown. Don't touch the fret wires. With your right hand strum slowly, making sure you hear each note clearly. The open strings help the chord ring out clearly.

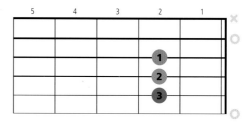

◀ C major
Place your fingers on the fingerboard as shown. Work to get your fingers to span all three frets evenly while still allowing the open strings to ring clearly. Strum with your right hand.

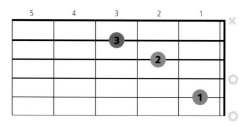

◀ E major

Place your fingers on the fingerboard as shown. Strum with the right hand and appreciate the very full ringing sound given by the three open strings.

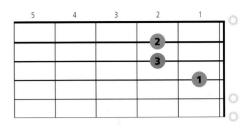

◀ G major

Place your fingers on the fingerboard as shown. Work on the stretch from the second finger to the third finger. Hear how the three open strings in the middle of the chord help the clarity of the sound.

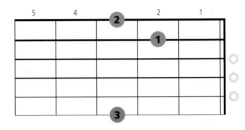

◀ D major

Position your left hand on the fingerboard as shown. Focus on the right hand: only strum four strings, as shown on the diagram. Give this lots of practice in preparation for changing chords quickly later.

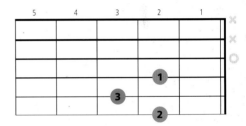

INTERMEDIATE MAJOR CHORDS TO PRACTISE

◀ B major

Place your fingers on the fingerboard as shown in the diagram. Pay extra attention to ensure each finger is in the correct place to prevent fret buzz. The B chord has no open strings.

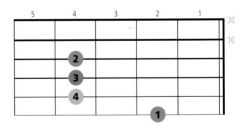

◀ F major

Place your fingers on the fingerboard as shown. Use a part barre (see page 17) by resting your first finger over the bottom two strings. Persevere with your strumming until both first finger notes ring clearly.

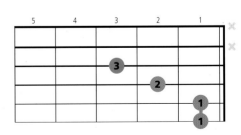

Basic MINOR CHORDS

Minor chords have an opposite sound to major chords: they often sound sad. Why is this? It's because the 3rd note in the grouping is 'flattened' (or one semitone lower in pitch than in a major chord). In guitar music minor chords are often indicated by an 'm' after the name of the chord. Here are seven more chords to practise. Start with the easy chords and move on to the intermediate chords, then the difficult chords. Memorize all the finger placings and chord names before you move on.

EASY MINOR CHORDS TO PRACTISE

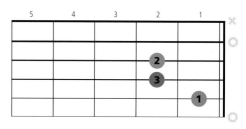

◀ A minor
Place your left-hand fingers on the fingerboard as shown and strum. Notice how similar this shape is to E major (see page 27), just moved down a string. Remember the shapes your fingers make for each chord. Group like with like, then remember the chord names.

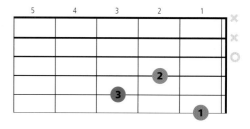

◀ D minor
Place your left hand on the fingerboard as shown, three fingers in three different frets. With your right hand make sure you strum just four strings. This makes this chord sound slightly emptier than a six-string chord.

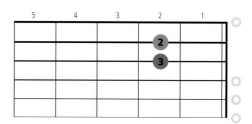

◀ E minor
Place your fingers on the fingerboard as shown, fretting two strings only. Hear how full-sounding the chord is, as it contains four open strings. This is possibly the saddest-sounding chord; commit it to memory for song-writing.

INTERMEDIATE MINOR CHORDS TO PRACTISE

◀ B minor

Place your fingers on the fingerboard as shown. Pay attention to the spreading of four fingers over three frets. Strum only four strings, as with D major. Since none of them are open, it can take practice to get the chord to ring clearly.

◀ C minor

As you position your fingers on the fingerboard notice how this chord is almost identical to the B minor chord, but played one fret higher up the fingerboard. Since it has no open strings, press the notes down firmly to avoid fret buzz.

DIFFICULT MINOR CHORDS TO PRACTISE

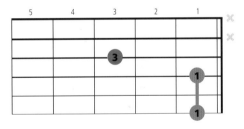

◀ F minor

Position your left-hand fingers, barring the bottom three strings in the 1st fret while arching your third finger over to fret the D string at the 3rd fret. It takes a great deal of practice to master this chord. Take it slowly and don't expect instant results.

◀ G minor

Position your left-hand fingers as shown, noting how your fingers make the same shape as F minor but moved up, so your first finger barres the 3rd fret. Since the frets are narrower here, the distance your fingers have to stretch is less.

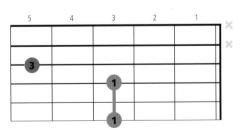

Basic SEVENTH CHORDS

What makes a seventh chord distinct? The 8th note in the major scale, or run of notes, is 'flattened' or lowered in pitch, in this case by one *whole tone* less than it would be in a major chord. You might find this note referred to as the minor 7th, ♭7, or dominant 7th, and it gives the chord its name as well as its distinctive sound. When looking at music, spot seventh chords by the 7 after the name of the chord. Here are some seventh chords to practise.

EASY SEVENTH CHORDS TO PRACTISE

◀ **A7**
Place your left-hand fingers on the fingerboard, as shown. Note the difference in position of your second finger from the A major chord (see page 26). It has been removed to sound the open G string (this is the 7th note in the octave, one tone down from the A).

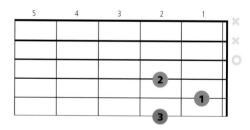

◀ **D7**
Position your left-hand fingers as shown. See how they reverse the shape of the D major chord (see page 27). As you practise, work to memorize both shapes to avoid confusion.

◀ **E7**
Position your left-hand fingers, seeing again how closely they resemble the position in the E major chord (see page 27). You simply remove your third finger to leave the D string open. When strumming make sure all the strings ring clearly, especially the open strings.

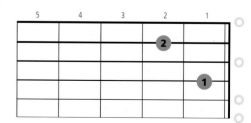

◀ G7

Position your left hand as shown, being wary of all the open strings. It is quite a stretch from the first finger to the third, so make sure you do not dampen any strings.

INTERMEDIATE SEVENTH CHORDS TO PRACTISE

◀ B7

Position your left hand, making sure all four fingers fit well: three fingers on non-adjacent strings in one fret can be a tight squeeze. With the right hand pay attention to allowing the B string to ring clearly.

◀ C7

Position your left hand, seeing how it is almost identical to the C major chord, except your fourth finger is on the 3rd fret of the G string (giving B♭, the 7th note). Practise until you get this right.

DIFFICULT SEVENTH CHORD TO PRACTISE

◀ F7

Position your left hand, using the first finger to barre across four strings, as shown. Place your second finger on the G string at the 2nd fret to cancel out the note which the first finger is barring.

JARGON BUSTER

Whole tone On the fingerboard a whole tone is two frets apart.

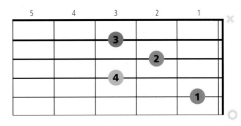

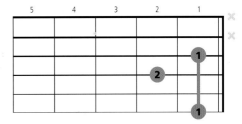

Basic MINOR SEVENTH CHORDS

Minor seventh chords are to minor chords what dominant seventh chords are to major chords. The 8th note in the minor scale, or run of notes, is 'flattened' or lowered in pitch by one whole tone. They are abbreviated to m7 in guitar music. Here are seven minor seventh chords to practise. Start with the easy ones. When you feel comfortable with these move on to the more challenging intermediate and difficult chords. Take time to fret every note correctly and strum only those strings necessary. Memorize all the finger placings and chord names before moving on to the next lesson.

EASY MINOR SEVENTH CHORDS TO PRACTISE

◀ **Am7**
Position your left-hand as shown on the diagram. See how the finger shape resembles the E7 chord, just moved down a string. Strum carefully to avoid sounding the 6th string. Focus on letting the open strings ring freely.

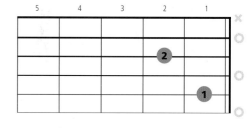

◀ **Bm7**
Position your fingers as shown. Strum without touching the two E strings, which change the sound of the chord completely. Practise strumming the middle four strings only.

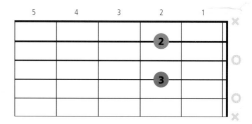

◀ **Em7**
Position your fingers as shown and enjoy the simplicity of the fingering, with one finger fretting the 2nd fret of the A string and the remaining strings played open.

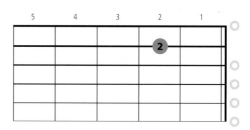

INTERMEDIATE MINOR SEVENTH CHORD TO PRACTISE

◀ Dm7

Position your fingers, noting how similar this chord is to the F major chord. Make sure you remove the third finger to release the open D string. Lay down your first finger firmly so both notes sound clearly.

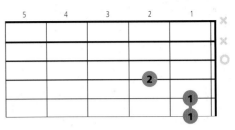

DIFFICULT MINOR SEVENTH CHORDS TO PRACTISE

◀ Cm7

Position your fingers carefully. Barre the first finger in the 1st fret and stretch over to the 3rd fret with your third and fourth fingers. With the right hand be careful only to strum the middle four strings.

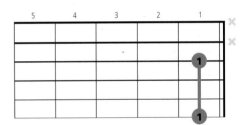

◀ Fm7

Position the one finger as shown, moving it around to find a position that allows all the notes to ring clearly.

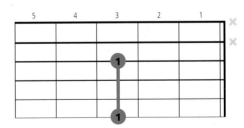

◀ Gm7

Position your left hand, noting how the finger shape almost replicates Fm7, but fretting in the 3rd fret. It takes a lot of practise to get this right.

Basic MAJOR SEVENTH CHORDS

Major seventh chords have a unique sound. The difference between major chords and major seventh chords is that the 8th note in the scale – the octave – is flattened by half a tone. Compare it to dominant seventh chords (see pages 30–31) where the octave is flattened by a whole tone. Major seventh chords are written in guitar music either as maj7 or as △7 (the triangle represents major). Here are some major seventh chords to practise.

EASY MAJOR SEVENTH CHORDS TO PRACTISE

◀ Amaj7 (A△7)
Position your left hand as shown. Compare the shape to the A major chord (see page 26). Your first finger on the 1st fret of the G string plays a note a semitone lower than in the major chord. This is what makes it a major seventh chord. This shape is also like a D7 chord moved up a string.

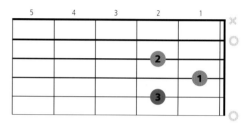

◀ Cmaj7 (C△7)
Position your left hand, noticing how similar the finger shape is to the C major chord. Remove your first finger to let the B string ring open as you strum. This is possibly the nicest sounding major seventh chord.

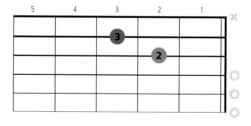

◀ Dmaj7 (D△7)
Position your fingers as shown, in the same finger pattern as for the A major chord but moved down a string. Play either with three separate fingers or by laying your first finger across all three notes.

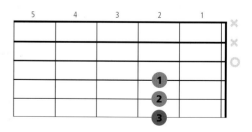

◂ Fmaj7 (F△7)

Position your fingers in a shape very similar to F major, but lift your first finger off the 1st string to let it ring open. When strumming pay attention to this string. The note must sound clearly because it is the major seventh and so defines the character of the chord.

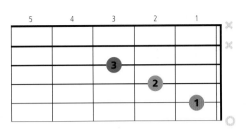

INTERMEDIATE MAJOR SEVENTH CHORDS TO PRACTISE

◂ Bmaj7 (B△7)

Position your left hand. It may take a little effort to get the three fingers into a comfortable position. It is important to deaden the 1st string; if it rings clearly it gives the chord a discordant tone.

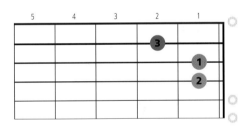

◂ Emaj7 (E△7)

Position your left hand as shown. It can be tricky squeezing your first and second fingers into the 1st fret while maintaining your third finger on the 2nd fret of the A string. The elevated position of the third finger can feel a little uncomfortable. With work it will soon seem natural.

◂ Gmaj7 (G△7)

Position your fingers as shown, seeing how by placing your first finger in the 2nd fret rather than in the 3rd or 1st this chord is a cross between G major and G7 (see pages 27 and 31). Twist your wrist to fit all three fingers into the correct frets. Practice makes this easier to master.

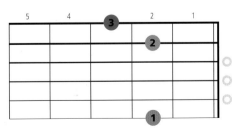

CHANGING chords

Now you can play a few chords, let's look at how to link them together, or change between chords. Some chords lend themselves easily to this; others might hold up the pace of a tune if you don't feel confident. Confidence, of course, comes with practice.

TOP TIP

Look for quick and easy finger movements between chords, where you can leave one or more fingers in place throughout the change. Memorize easy changes, so that one chord reminds you of others that are easily linked to it.

CHANGING CHORDS

The easiest way into this is to look for and memorize links between chords, so that you cut back on finger movement. This makes for smooth changes. As you worked through the chords on pages 26–35, you should already have started grouping similar finger patterns. Here are some exercises to develop speed and dexterity. When you have committed them to memory, experiment with other chords to see how many more easy changes you can find.

EASY EXERCISES TO PRACTISE

◀ C to F
Play C major and change to F major, leaving your first finger in place and moving the second and third fingers down a string.

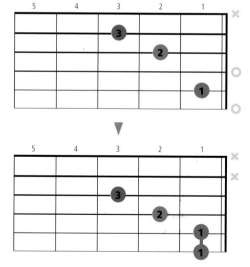

◀ E to Am

Play an E chord and change to an Am chord by moving all fingers down one string.

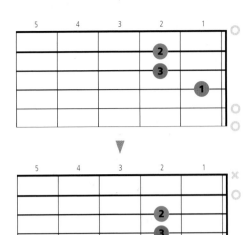

◀ A7 to Bm7

Play an A7 chord and change to a Bm7 chord by moving all fingers up a string. You can use either your first or second finger to fret the D and A strings.

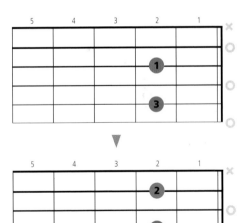

TIMING and STRUMMING

Strumming and timing patterns are also vital in linking chords. Practise the exercises below, which progress in difficulty. As ever, don't move on until you have mastered every exercise. Playing in time is important if you want to play with other musicians.

TIMING CHARTS

These show what chords to play and how many beats each chord lasts for. Further beats are shown by a / symbol, so 'Bm / / /' means you play B minor chord for four beats. Try out the exercises below, strumming one down stroke for each beat. All three tunes have four beats in a bar, known as $\frac{4}{4}$ time. Though this is the most common timing you will encounter, there could be any number of beats in a bar.

> ### KEY TO CHART
>
> | Bar line ||: :|| Repeat marks: repeat everything in this section.

PROGRESSION EXERCISES

Progression 1
This progression uses easy chords. Work through it slowly and don't move on until you can play it confidently.

||: C / / / | E / / / | Am / / / | Am7 / / / | Dm / / / | G / / / | Cmaj7 / / / | G7 / / / :||

Progression 2
Now bring in some intermediate chords. Again, practise until you can play these with fluency and confidence.

||: G / / / | Bm / / / | Em / / / | Em7 / / / | C7 / / / | D / / / | C7 / / / | D7 / / / :||

Progression 3
Several of the chords in this sequence are rated difficult. Don't attempt this sequence until you have mastered the earlier ones.

||: Cm / / / | Fm / / / | Gm / / / | Cm / / / | Fm7 / / / | Gm7 / / / | Fm7 / / / | Gm7 / / / :||

▲ A metronome can be used to ensure that you keep in time. Digital or analogue, these can be set up to tap out any 'bpm' (beats per minute).

STRUMMING PATTERNS

The four beats in each bar in the tunes you have just practised refer to the pulse of the piece. As long as you keep to the pulse (tap your foot as you play), you can strum as many or as few beats as you like: a combination of down and up strokes can sound really effective and change the rhythmic feel. Now try some strumming exercises. They use only an A chord so that you focus on the right, not the left hand. A downward strum is signified by a V, an upward strum by the symbol ^. Note that strums are not always played on the beat.

STRUMMING EXERCISES

Strumming 1

Start slowly and don't speed up or move on until you know the piece well.

```
     V    V   V^V  V    V    V^V  V    V^V  V   V^V^V   V
||:  A   /   /   /  | A   /   /   /  | A   /   /   /  | A   /   /   /  :||
```

Strumming 2

Once you have mastered this sequence, progress to the final exercise.

```
   V ^ V ^ V          V   V^V^V  V       V  V^ V   V   V^V
||:  A   /   /   /  | A   /   /   /  | A   /   /   /  | A   /   /   /  :||
```

Strumming 3

This progression only has three beats in a bar, known as $\frac{3}{4}$ time. Tap it out before adding chords to get accustomed to the different pattern.

```
     V    V    V    V    V ^ V   V ^ V    V    V    V    V
||:  A   /   /  | D   /   /  | E   /   /  | D   /   /  |
```

```
   V ^ V ^ V    V      V ^ V   V    V ^ V^ V    V    V
|  A   /   /  | D   /   /  | E   /   /  | D   /   /  :||
```

MOVING ON

Now revise the three progression exercises, experimenting with some different strumming patterns. Start with a very basic pattern and make it more complex as your confidence grows.

FINGER PICKING and ROOT NOTES

A slightly more advanced way of playing chords is to finger pick. In this technique you pick out the root note of the chord (usually the lowest note) with your right thumb and then use your fingers either to pick or strum through the remaining notes. In hybrid finger picking you use a plectrum instead of your thumb, holding it between thumb and first finger as normal, then use the remaining three fingers to pick the strings. Finger picking can be used to great effect in any style of music, although it is most often heard in country and folk music. To be able to play this style you have to be able to identify the root note of each chord.

HOW TO FIND THE ROOT NOTE

The root note, the note that gives the chord its name and distinct group of notes, is commonly the lowest note in a chord. But it isn't always. In chords where the root note has been displaced because of the positioning of fingers (and figures higher in the chord's layout) you can generally use the lowest note in the chord to start the finger pick. It is important to begin with a low note so the finger-picking pattern has a nice progressive flow.

EASY EXERCISES

▶ **A chord**
Play an A major chord, making the first note you play with thumb or plectrum the 5th string (the A string provides this chord's root note). With your other fingers pick down through the chord to the 1st string and back up again.

▶ **C chord**
Play a C major chord, again starting at the 5th string with thumb or plectrum and picking to the 1st string and back with your other fingers.

▶ **D chord**
Now pick through a D major chord, this time starting at the 4th string (the D string provides this chord's root note). Pick to the 1st string and back.

CHORD PATTERN EXERCISES

Chord pattern 1
Once you have mastered the art of picking strings with the right-hand fingers, try playing this chord pattern. If the root note has been displaced, pick from the lowest note in the chord to the highest.

‖: G / / / | B / / / | Em / / / | Em7 / / / | Am / / / | D / / / | Gmaj7 / / / | D7 / / / :‖

Chord pattern 2
Move on to this pattern when you can confidently play the previous one.

‖: C / / / | Em / / / | Am / / / | Am7 / / / | F / / / | G / / / | F / / / | G7 / / / :‖

Chord pattern 3
Tackle this pattern last.

‖: Dm / / / | Gm / / / | Dm / / / | Dm / / / | Gm7 / / / | Am7 / / / | Gm7 / / / | Am7 / / / :‖

LESSON SUMMARY

You have studied, practised and memorized the finger positions and names of 35 chords in total. Some you will use a lot; others you may never use. Either way, you must learn them all as they represent a solid knowledge of basic chord groups and the way they fit together. After mastering the chord shapes with the left hand, you moved on to the right hand, learning strumming and finger picking. Separating the hands is a good way to work. If you work on both hands simultaneously it takes longer to master the guitar and the sound you make is less impressive.

LESSON 4 BASIC MUSIC THEORY

AIM TO UNDERSTAND THE MOST
IMPORTANT AREAS OF MUSIC THEORY
FOR A GUITARIST. THIS CHAPTER IS A
RESOURCE TO DIP INTO WHILE YOU ARE
WORKING THROUGH THE OTHER MORE
'HANDS-ON' CHAPTERS.

If you aspire to play with other musicians, write songs, become a
session guitarist or lead a band you will need to know something
about the theory of music. In this chapter you will learn how to
read music, understand how to transfer it to your fingerboard and
get a grounding in how notes relate to each other.

How to READ MUSIC

Standard music notation is the form most often used by musicians for writing down their
ideas. Understanding the principles benefits you as a musician. Although this is a very
common music form, it isn't necessarily the easiest way for a guitarist to learn music; other
methods, such as tablature (see pages 116–19), are much more effective.

WHAT DO THE SYMBOLS MEAN?

Music is most commonly written on five lines and the spaces between them, a
framework known as a staff. Each line and space corresponds to a different pitch.
Notes for high-pitched instruments are indicated by a treble clef symbol: 𝄞. Notes
for lower-pitched instruments are shown with the bass clef symbol: 𝄢. Guitar
music is most commonly notated on the treble staff, so this will be our focus.

ALL ABOUT NOTES

Western music sounds like it does because it's based on a grouping of 12
different notes, all separated by an interval called a semitone, or half-step. This
group of notes is called an octave. The pattern of 12-note octaves is like a cycle
and continues on indefinitely. It is easy to see how the notes are laid out on a
piano keyboard.

► The white notes on a piano are named from A to G; the black notes represent sharps (#) and flats (♭). As you can see, the black notes each have two possible names, depending on if they are sharpened from below or flattened from above. For this reason they are called 'enharmonic' notes. A key signature written at the start of a piece of music indicates which name you use and when you use it (see pages 48–50).

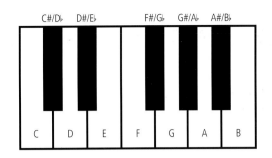

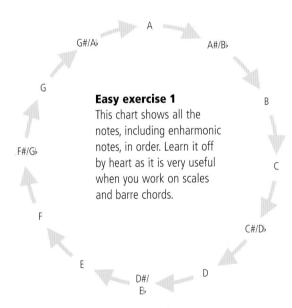

Easy exercise 1
This chart shows all the notes, including enharmonic notes, in order. Learn it off by heart as it is very useful when you work on scales and barre chords.

▼ **Easy exercise 2**
Here is the treble staff with all the notes named that sit on the lines and in the spaces. The extra short lines below and above the standard five are called ledger lines. Notes have ascending tails when at the bottom of the stave and descending tails at the top of the stave. Learn the names of the notes and ask someone to test you on them. Use the phrase **E**very **G**ood **B**oy **D**eserves **F**ood to help you remember the notes on the lines, **FACE** to give you the notes in the spaces. For flats and sharps you will see ♭ or # written just before the note.

HOW DOES THIS RELATE TO THE GUITAR?

This diagram shows the fingerboard of the guitar with all notes written on it. Using this you can work out where any notes from a staff are on the guitar. Notice how the cycle of notes can be traced on every string by following the pattern up the fingerboard. Practise playing runs of notes to hear the cycle.

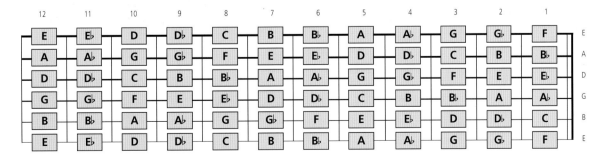

TEMPO and RHYTHM

The tempo of a piece of music determines how fast it is played, and the rhythm is the 'feel' or 'groove' of the piece. Two tunes played at the same tempo, but with a different rhythm sound completely unrelated. Tempo is usually measured in beats per minute (bpm) with 120 bpm being most commonly used.

WHAT DO THE TERMS MEAN?

This chart shows the equivalent bpm for the Italian terms used to indicate tempo on musical scores. Look at the variation in the suggested bpm for each tempo mark: it's up to the conductor or player to decide how fast or slow a piece is played. It is worth remembering these terms.

TEMPO TERMINOLOGY		
MUSICAL TERM	PACE	APPROX. BPM
Grave	Very very slow	Below 40 bpm
Lento	Very slow	40–55 bpm
Largo	Slow	45–65 bpm
Adagio	Slow (at ease)	55–75 bpm
Andante	Walking speed	75–105 bpm
Moderato	Moderate speed	105–120 bpm
Allegro	Fast	120–160 bpm
Vivace	Lively	150–170 bpm
Presto	Very fast	170–210 bpm
Prestissimo	Very very fast	210+ bpm

WHAT DICTATES THE RHYTHM?

The feel of the piece and style of music influences its rhythm. For example, a slow ballad requires a slow rhythm pattern while an up-tempo Latin tune needs a faster rhythm with more accented notes. Rhythm guitar playing is the art of strumming or picking chords, whilst keeping in time with the tempo. We saw in Lesson 3 (pages 38–39) how to vary strumming patterns to create interesting rhythm patterns using up and down strokes.

LEARNING NOTE VALUES

If you understand what type of beat each musical note represents, you'll be better equipped to write songs and guitar solos. The chart below shows all the main note values and the symbols that represent them on a staff. They vary from a note which is sustained over four beats, to a note which lasts one sixty-fourth of a beat, and are all shown here on one bar of music with four beats. American versions of the name follow the English description. Try and clap the notes while tapping out four beats with your foot.

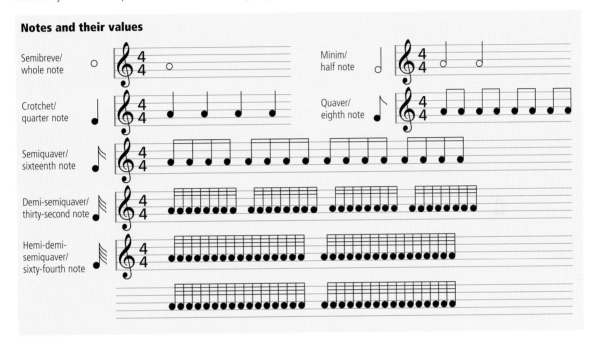

Notes and their values

Semibreve/ whole note

Crotchet/ quarter note

Semiquaver/ sixteenth note

Demi-semiquaver/ thirty-second note

Hemi-demi-semiquaver/ sixty-fourth note

Minim/ half note

Quaver/ eighth note

WHEN THERE ARE NO NOTES

A rest sign on a musical staff shows where there is to be a gap in a piece of music and is an indication not to play. Rests tie in with note values: different symbols tell the musician not to play for the length of time that the note would have lasted had it been written. In this chart the symbols are shown and written out in a bar of music. Notice how the flags attached to the stalks of the quaver notes and rests correspond. For example, a semiquaver has two flags and so does a sixteenth note rest because it has the same time value. When joined together on the staff the flags on quaver notes turn into beams.

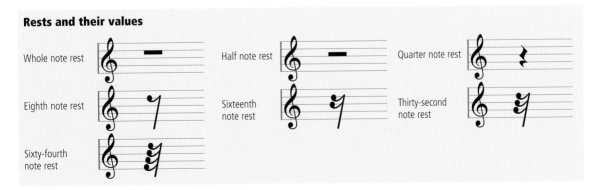

Rests and their values

Whole note rest

Eighth note rest

Sixty-fourth note rest

Half note rest

Sixteenth note rest

Quarter note rest

Thirty-second note rest

TIME signatures

Written at the start of a piece of music, time signatures tell us how many beats there are in each bar, or rhythmic sub-division, of the tune, and what type of beats they are. Most popular music is written in $\frac{4}{4}$ time, which represents four crotchet beats to a bar.

READING TIME SIGNATURES

Look at the first line of a piece of music. Before any notes on the staff there will be two numbers, one above the other. Most often it will be $\frac{4}{4}$, which means there are four crotchet beats in each bar. This is sometimes referred to as common time and signified by a C in the place of the time signature. The number shown on top represents the number of beats in the bar; the number on the bottom signifies the type of beat (2 for a minim, 4 for crotchets, 8 for quavers). The value of all the notes in each bar has to add up to the number on the top of the time signature. The important thing to remember is that minim beats are counted slower than crotchet beats, and that crotchet beats are counted slower than quaver beats.

Time signatures that you might see

$\frac{2}{2}$ 2 minim beats per bar, so all notes in each bar have to add up to two.

$\frac{6}{4}$ 6 crotchet beats per bar, so the total of notes in the bar must be six.

$\frac{12}{8}$ 12 quaver beats per bar, again the total value of notes must be 12.

Counting exercise

1 Take $\frac{4}{4}$ time and count it out loud, following the diagram: 1 2 3 4.

2 Now add a 2 and a 3 after each count to give a count of: 1(23), 2(23), 3(23), 4(23).

Notice how each count is now grouped as a triplet, effectively making 12 beats instead of four. Because we usually have to count the beats quicker to fit them all in, the counts become quaver beats, changing the time signature from $\frac{4}{4}$ to $\frac{12}{8}$.

COMPOUND TIME SIGNATURES

In simple time, seen opposite, the beat divides into two units. In compound time, the beat divides into three sub-units. We can create a compound time signature by adding triplets to any crotchet beat time signature, as we saw in step 2 of the exercise above.

Changing 2/4 time

1 Here is a bar of standard $\frac{2}{4}$ time.

2 Add crotchet triplets and the time signature becomes $\frac{6}{4}$ time.

3 Substitute quaver triplets and the time signature becomes $\frac{6}{8}$ time.

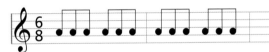

Changing 3/4 time

1 Here is a bar of standard $\frac{3}{4}$ time.

2 Add crotchet triplets and it becomes $\frac{9}{4}$ time.

3 Turn them into quaver triplets and it becomes $\frac{9}{8}$ time.

Changing 4/4 time

1 Here is a bar of standard $\frac{4}{4}$ time.

2 Add crotchet triplets and it becomes $\frac{12}{4}$ time.

3 Substitute quaver triplets and it becomes $\frac{12}{8}$ time.

ASYMMETRIC TIME SIGNATURES

In these time signatures the number of beats in each bar is not divisible by two or three. Most commonly there are five or seven beats per bar, and occasionally eleven or thirteen, usually accented so they can be broken down into easily playable segments. Such time signatures are generally considered strange, though if you like jazz, you'll be familiar with them perhaps without knowing. In popular music, Sting uses asymmetric time signatures to great effect.

Listening exercise

Listen to 'Take Five' by Paul Desmond and Dave Brubeck. This tune is in $\frac{5}{4}$: five crotchet beats per bar. But the five beats are divided into a two and a three, so the count for one bar could be either 123, 12 or 12, 123. Try to count along. It is common to accent certain beats in an asymmetric time signature; an accent is marked on the staff by ^ above the beat.

5/4 time

KEY signatures

After the treble clef sign and time signature at the start of a piece of music you will often see some sharp and flat signs written on the staff. They are a key signature and tell the musician what group of notes, or key, the piece of music uses.

WHAT ARE KEY SIGNATURES?

The notes of the melody of a song are taken by the musician not randomly, but from set groupings, or scales. The root note of a scale gives the scale its name, or key. So by looking at the notes in a melody we can identify the key of the piece of music. If the notes are taken from the C major scale, the song is said to be in the key of C major and has a key signature of C.

TYPES OF KEY

Keys come in two types, sharp (#) and flat (♭). This is determined by the notes that make up the major scale. For example, G major is a sharp key because its major scale has F# in it. The key of G is signified on a staff by a # symbol written on the F line (see diagram below). The tables below set out all the key signatures and which sharp or flat notes they contain. You will notice some notes not on your guitar – E#, B#, C♭, F♭ are usually called F, C, B, E, but in key signatures have pseudonyms to fit with the pattern of sharps or flats.

Sharp key signatures

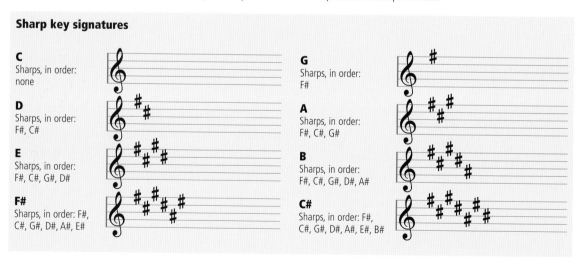

C
Sharps, in order:
none

D
Sharps, in order:
F#, C#

E
Sharps, in order:
F#, C#, G#, D#

F#
Sharps, in order: F#,
C#, G#, D#, A#, E#

G
Sharps, in order:
F#

A
Sharps, in order:
F#, C#, G#

B
Sharps, in order:
F#, C#, G#, D#, A#

C#
Sharps, in order: F#,
C#, G#, D#, A#, E#, B#

Flat key signatures

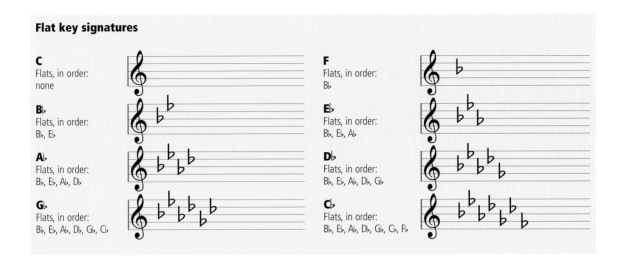

C
Flats, in order:
none

B♭
Flats, in order:
B♭, E♭

A♭
Flats, in order:
B♭, E♭, A♭, D♭

G♭
Flats, in order:
B♭, E♭, A♭, D♭, G♭, C♭

F
Flats, in order:
B♭

E♭
Flats, in order:
B♭, E♭, A♭

D♭
Flats, in order:
B♭, E♭, A♭, D♭, G♭

C♭
Flats, in order:
B♭, E♭, A♭, D♭, G♭, C♭, F♭

ON THE STAFF

Sharps and flats crop up in written music when not featured as part of the key signature. The symbol is written next to the note to be sharpened or flattened, and is known as an 'accidental'. An accidental is only valid for one bar and a return to the standard note within the bar is marked by a 'natural' sign (♮).

CIRCLE OF FIFTHS

▶ The key of C has no sharps or flats and each key moving away from it gains one sharp or flat at a time. This relationship of keys can be set out visually as a circle of fifths. The circle has 12 segments with the key of C at the top. Move clockwise around the circle in intervals of a fifth and you find each major scale differs from the preceding scale by one note. This is where key signatures come from. The diagram also highlights 5th and 4th notes (or intervals) in each major scale. To find a 5th move around the circle clockwise (for example in the scale of G it is D); for a 4th move anticlockwise (for example, in the scale of C it is F).

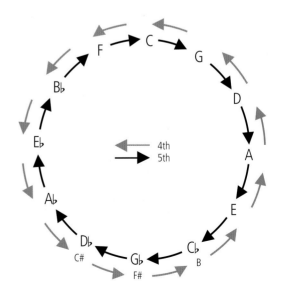

SHARPS AND FLATS READY RECKONER

If you find key signatures daunting, use this easy method to work them out on the guitar. Place your fingers in the same finger shape in various positions on the neck to see the keys in order and the sharp and flat notes that make up those keys.

To find sharp keys

Place your fingers in the following position on the 7th and 8th frets. This gives you the sharp keys C – G – D – A – E – B. Descend from high C to low F# on the 2nd fret.

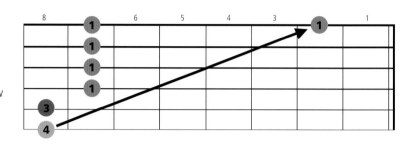

To find flat keys

Maintaining the hand position, move your fingers one fret higher, to the 8th and 9th frets. This gives the flat keys C – F – B♭ – E♭ – A♭ – D♭. Ascend from low C to high G♭ on the 14th fret.

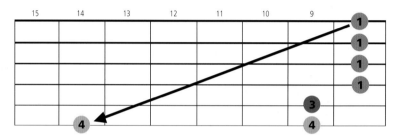

To find the sharps in order

With fingers still in the same position, move up to the 1st and 2nd frets to see the sharps in order: F# – C# – G# – D# – A# – E#. Descend from high F# to low E#.

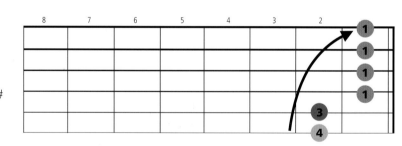

To find the flats in order

Move your fingers, maintaining the hand position, to the 6th and 7th frets to see the flats in order: B♭ – E♭ – A♭ – D♭ – G♭ – C♭. Ascend from low B♭ to high C♭.

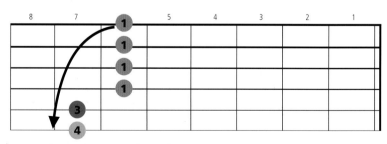

VOLUME

Loudness in music is largely determined by the type of piece being played: a slow ballad, for example, is usually much quieter than a heavy metal song. A series of Italian words on written music known as 'dynamic markings' tell us how loudly or softly to play. They are written above the music to indicate where they apply and vary throughout the song.

TOP TIP

When given a piece of music, study it carefully before starting to play, making sure you are aware of any rhythmic or volume changes. Failure to do this can leave you floundering halfway through a piece or performance.

DYNAMIC MARKINGS		
SYMBOL	TERM	MEANING
ppp	Pianississimo	As softly as possible
pp	Pianissimo	Very softly
p	Piano	Softly
mp	Mezzo-Piano	Moderately softly
m	Mezzo	Medium (Mezzo = half)
mf	Mezzo-Forte	Moderately loudly
f	Forte	Loudly
ff	Fortissimo	Very loudly
fff	Fortississimo	As loudly as possible
pf	Piu forte	More loudly
fp	Fortepiano	Sudden change from loud to soft
cresc. or <	Crescendo	Gradually become louder
dim. or >	Decrescendo (Diminuendo)	Gradually become softer

DYNAMICS EXERCISE

Play these two chord charts, which have many dynamic marks to follow. Work on increasing or decreasing volume smoothly and evenly. Don't move on to the second chart until you feel happy playing the first chart.

Chart 1

```
     p              mf          m         f        ff       p
||: C / / / |Am / / / |F / / / |G / / / |C / / / |Am7 / / / |F / / / |G7 / / / :||
```

Chart 2

```
     fff            ppp      p         m        mf              ff
||: A / / / |D / / / |A / / / |A7 / / / |E7 / / / |D7 / / / |A / / / |E7 / / / :||
```

CADENCES

A cadence is a set series of chords or notes that end a phrase, section or an entire piece of music. There are four types of cadence, which give musical phrases a distinctive ending that can indicate whether the piece is continuing or to be concluded, and are formed by combining two notes or chords.

PERFECT CADENCE
This is perhaps the most common cadence and usually signifies the end of the piece as it gives a very definite impression of resolution. It moves from the 5th note in the scale to the 1st, or key note, the one that gives the scale its name. In the key of C the move would be from G to C – the dominant or 5th note to the tonic or root note (written as V to I).

PLAGAL CADENCE
Often referred to as the Amen cadence because this is what it sounds like, this set of notes also resolves to the 1st, or tonic, note of the scale. But it sounds less definite because it is preceded by the 4th note in the scale, known as the subdominant. In the key of C the move would be from F to C (written as IV to I).

IMPERFECT CADENCE
Any cadence ending on the 5th note of the scale (written as V) is called imperfect. It can be preceded by any other note, usually the 2nd (II), 4th (IV) or 1st (I) note of the scale. In the key of C it would have to land on the 5th, or dominant, note, G.

INTERRUPTED CADENCE
Perhaps the most unusual cadence, this starts on the 5th (V) note of the scale, the dominant, and lands on any note except the 1st. It usually ends on the 6th note, the submediant (VI), but this isn't always so. In the key of C, the 5th note G would generally be followed by Am, but it could be any note except C.

How notes RELATE

All notes on the fingerboard relate to one another and the way in which they do this is determined by the key you play in. Although it's a complex matter, it's vital to understand this theory if you dream of becoming a serious musician.

DIATONIC NOTE RELATIVITY

The word diatonic means using only the seven tones of a standard major scale (omitting the extra semitone gradations of pitch known as chromatic notes). The major scale, as with all scales, follows a set pattern of notes. All these notes are relative to one another and are referred to as intervals. Intervals are measured either in semitones (half-steps) or whole tones (steps). On a guitar a semitone is the distance between one fret; a whole tone the distance between two frets. The first note of any scale is called the root, or tonic, and all other notes in the scale are relative to this.

Numbering a scale

The C major scale features the notes C, D, E, F, G, A, B – all the white notes on a piano. Let's number them from the 1st to the 7th note, as shown on the piano keyboard below. All the notes relate to the 1st, or root, note and each one has two names that relate it to the root note. You'll find those names in the chart below. If you continue the pattern, note 8 repeats the root note but at a higher pitch. This is called the octave.

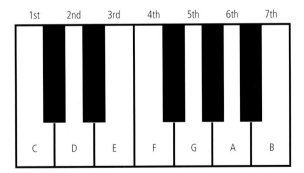

NAMES OF NOTES						
ROOT OR TONIC	MAJOR 2ND OR SUPERTONIC	MAJOR 3RD OR MEDIANT	PERFECT 4TH OR SUBDOMINANT	PERFECT 5TH OR DOMINANT	MAJOR 6TH OR SUBMEDIANT	MAJOR 7TH OR LEADING NOTE
1st	2nd	3rd	4th	5th	6th	7th

Recognizing patterns

The note names tell us how the notes relate to each other in the major scale, but not about their proximity to one another. To gain this knowledge we need to memorize the interval pattern in the chart below, which shows how all the notes in a major scale fall in relation to each other. See how the interval between the 1st and the 2nd note is a whole tone, like the interval between the 2nd and 3rd notes. Look at how the interval between other notes, such as the 3rd and 4th, is a semitone. The best part is that this pattern isn't exclusive to the key of C, it can be used on any starting note. Once you know the root note you can work out any major scale by following this interval pattern. One of the nicest things about guitar is that it is transpositional, meaning simply that by moving left-hand finger shapes around the fingerboard you can play in different keys. A major scale at the 8th fret is C, whereas the same finger pattern at the 3rd fret gives you a G major scale. You don't have to learn loads of finger patterns for each scale, as a pianist does!

INTERVAL PATTERNS							
1ST	2ND	3RD	4TH	5TH	6TH	7TH	(8TH/1ST)
	tone	tone	semitone	tone	tone	tone	semitone

Easy exercise

1 Let's put this information on to the neck of the guitar. Here is a one octave C major scale starting on the 6th string. Play it through slowly, thinking about each note you are playing, and you will notice how the interval pattern works.

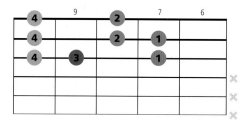

2 Move the root note, maintaining the same finger pattern. Start on the 3rd fret – now you are playing a G major scale.

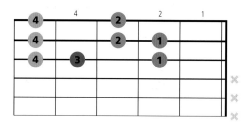

3 Now see if you can play another major scale, in a different key, simply by moving your fingers to start on another fret.

Chord formula

You can play chords that tie in with the above pattern by learning another formula made up of major and minor chords: a diatonic chord pattern. The chord shapes are set out on the bottom line of the chart. Try to memorize it (don't worry about the tricky chord names). Also shown is a diatonic chord pattern for the key of C.

DIATONIC CHORD PATTERN						
1ST	2ND	3RD	4TH	5TH	6TH	7TH
Major	Minor	Minor	Major	Major	Minor	Minor
maj7	m7	m7	maj7#11	7	m	m7♭5

DIATONIC CHORD PATTERN IN THE KEY OF C						
1ST	2ND	3RD	4TH	5TH	6TH	7TH
Cmaj7	Dm7	Em7	Fmaj7#11	G7	Am	Bm7♭5

UNDERSTANDING RELATIVE MAJOR AND MINOR INTERVALS

Once you grasp the following theory you'll find yourself spotting it used in all kinds of music. The 1st note of a major scale, the root (or tonic), also has a relative minor scale, found if you count up to the 6th note, or interval. In the key of C the tonic is C, so, counting upward, the relative minor is Am, shown below. Use the pattern in reverse, too by counting downward: the relative major of A minor is C.

RELATIVE MINOR INTERVAL PATTERN FOR AM						
6TH	7TH	1ST	2ND	3RD	4TH	5TH
Am	Bm7♭5	Cmaj7	Dm7	Em7	Fmaj7#11	G7

RELATIVE MAJOR/MINOR INTERVALS	
RELATIVE MAJOR	RELATIVE MINOR
A	F#m
A#/B♭	Gm
B	G#m
C	Am
C#/D♭	A#m
D	Bm
D#/E♭	Cm
E	C#m
F	Dm
F#/G♭	D#m
G	Em
G#/A♭	Fm

HOW IS THIS USEFUL?

Knowledge of diatonic note relativity is useful not least because it helps you understand how notes connect to one another. With this knowledge, you can find chords and notes that blend well together when writing chord patterns or solos. It's a failsafe option because these notes and chords always work.

The more simple reason for understanding diatonic note relativity is because chord patterns are often named as their interval position, and musicians are expected to be able to follow this. A bandleader might call out a tune as 'a 2–5–1 in C'. He means the first chord is the 2nd interval of the key of C (Dm7), the second chord is the 5th interval of C (G7) and the third chord is C itself. These intervals are often written as Roman numerals, so 2–5–1 would be II–V–I. Failure to understand this may get you kicked out of the band!

Chord PROGRESSIONS

Most musicians have heard of three-chord tricks and turnaround progressions, but many don't know what they are, so let's clear it up... A three-chord trick is a very common working example of diatonic note relativity (see pages 53–55). It is a piece of music, 12 bars in length, that repeats over and over and forms the basis of most blues and rock 'n' roll. You might know it as 12-bar blues. The question is how do you know which three chords to play? Once you have the formula of how to work out the chords and the order in which to play them, you can jam with musicians from all over the world. Another useful chord progression is the 'turnaround'. It takes its name because it is often used as the last four chords of a progression to lead a song neatly back to its beginning; the section of a tune often referred to as a turnaround.

TOP TIP

The dominant chord is usually played as a seventh (adding the 7th note in the scale), but this is not always the case. What is important is that you remember the pattern and practise using it widely, in all keys. Experiment with the formula; substituting majors with minors, for example, and adding and removing 7th notes. This adds colour to the sound of the piece, and helps extend your repertoire.

THE THREE-CHORD TRICK

The formula

The chords to play are these: the tonic, subdominant and dominant, or first, fourth and fifth to name them another way. Here is a chart to show you the order that the chords are played in, and for how many bars. Remember, there are four beats to the bar, and the pattern repeats over and over.

12-bar blues

	: tonic (1) / / /	subdominant (4) / / /	tonic (1) / / /	tonic (1) / / /
subdominant (4) / / /	subdominant (4) / / /	tonic (1) / / /	tonic (1) / / /
dominant (5) / / /	subdominant (4) / / /	tonic (1) / / /	dominant (5) / / / :	

12-bar blues exercise

Here is the same chart, but this time showing a three-chord trick in the key of C. Try playing it, remembering to tap four beats to the bar, and repeating the pattern over and over until it feels natural.

Three-chord trick in C

	: C (tonic) / / /	F (subdominant) / / /	C (tonic) / / /	C (tonic) / / /
F (subdominant) / / /	F (subdominant) / / /	C (tonic) / / /	C (tonic) / / /
G (dominant) / / /	F (subdominant) / / /	C (tonic) / / /	G (dominant) / / / :	

THE TURNAROUND PROGRESSION

The formula

In this instance the turnaround comprises the following chord intervals: tonic – submediant – subdominant – dominant, or 1–6–4–5. They are generally played for four beats each, with the dominant chord neatly leading back into the tonic at the end of each four bars.

Turnaround exercise

Try a turnaround in the key of C by playing the following chord progression. As you work through it try to commit the changes to memory and play without looking at the chart.

Turnaround in C

```
||: C   /   /   / | Am   /   /   / | F   /   /   / | G   /   /   / :||
```

Experimenting exercise

The more your chord knowledge improves as you work through the lessons, the more you should experiment with changing shapes. Try substituting the dominant chord for a seventh, or play the sixth as Am7, for instance. Don't be afraid of getting it wrong: this only leads to getting it right next time.

Chromatic note RELATIVITY

When looking at the diatonic relation of notes (see pages 53–55), we saw that notes are numbered according to their relation to each other from 1 to 7, with 8 becoming the octave. You might ask whether notes that are not in the diatonic note pattern relate to the root note too? The answer is yes. To find out what these notes are called, we need to learn about chromatic note relativity.

DEFINING CHROMATIC

The word chromatic means 'every note', so a chromatic scale uses every note between the root and octave notes. This gives a scale of 12 notes in every octave. Each of the 12 notes has a relative number to the root note of the key you are in. For ease of learning, we will use the key of A for all examples in this lesson.

It might seem logical to call the root note the 1st, and then to number each of the 12 notes in the chromatic scale from 1 to 12, with the octave being numbered 12. This, however, is not the case. Remember how the diatonic note pattern is numbered from 1 to 7 and the octave note is 8. In the chromatic note pattern the octave note has to remain as 8 (the prefix 'oct' means eight). Therefore, the 12 notes are numbered differently to incorporate the relative numbers of the diatonic interval pattern.

Why do I need to learn this?

Guitar students often look through song books or search the Internet for the chord patterns of favourite songs. Most inexperienced players ignore chords they don't know or, at best, use the nearest substitute they can find. If you fully understand chromatic note relativity, you can work out a version of any chord and need never use weak substitution chords.

THE CHROMATIC SCALE

The chromatic scale is formed by playing every note at a semitone interval. Here are the notes of the chromatic scale in one octave of the key of A. Below are the relative numbers of all the chromatic notes in this octave of the scale. From this we can see how we get from the root to the octave using 12 notes but still only ending up on 8. Look at the notes numbered 1 – 2 – 3 – 4 – 5 – 6 – 7 – 8 and see how they make up a major scale and also form the diatonic note pattern.

CHROMATIC SCALE IN A												
A	A#/B♭	B	C	C#/D♭	D	D#/E♭	E	F	F#/G♭	G	G#/A♭	A
1	♭2	2	♭3	3	4	♭5	5	♭6	6	♭7	7	8

NAMES AND NUMBERS

Now you recognize the chromatic note pattern, it's important to get to know some of the other names given to the number positions. Learn all the names and numbers to prepare you for all eventualities as a guitarist. Moving into the second octave brings note numbers above 8. An A13 chord, for example, suggests that you need to play the 13th note (here, F#), found only in the second octave. If you played an A13 chord but fretted the F# in the first octave, you would in effect be playing an A6 chord, because the F# in the first octave is the 6th note.

1ST OCTAVE NAMES AND NUMBERS

ROOT	♭2ND	2ND	MINOR 3RD	MAJOR 3RD	PERFECT 4TH	♭5TH	PERFECT 5TH	#5TH	6TH	MINOR/ DOMINANT	MAJOR 7TH	OCTAVE
A	A#/B♭	B	C	C#/D♭	D	D#/E♭	E	F	F#/G♭	G	G#/A♭	A

2ND OCTAVE NAMES AND NUMBERS

♭9TH	9TH	MINOR 10TH #9TH/ ♭10TH	MAJOR 10TH	PERFECT 11TH	#11TH	5TH	♭13TH	13TH	MINOR/ DOMINANT 7TH	MAJOR 7TH	(DOUBLE) OCTAVE
A#/B♭	B	C	C#/D♭	D	D#/E♭	E	F	F#/G♭	G	G#/A♭	A

PUTTING IT INTO PRACTICE

Knowing the theory of diatonic and chromatic note relativity is all very well, but it isn't much use if you have no way of putting it into practice on the fingerboard. There are lots of versions of the same note on a guitar, so there is more than one position for each interval in relation to the root note. Let's take A as the root and show all the main intervals available to it.

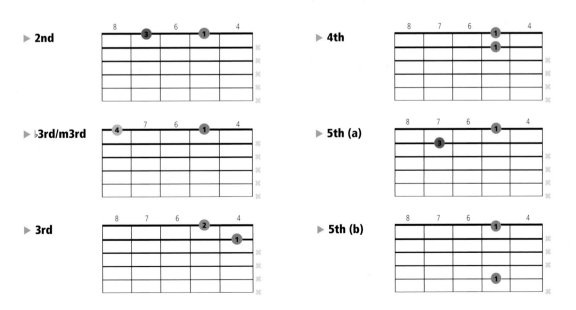

▶ 2nd

▶ ♭3rd/m3rd

▶ 3rd

▶ 4th

▶ 5th (a)

▶ 5th (b)

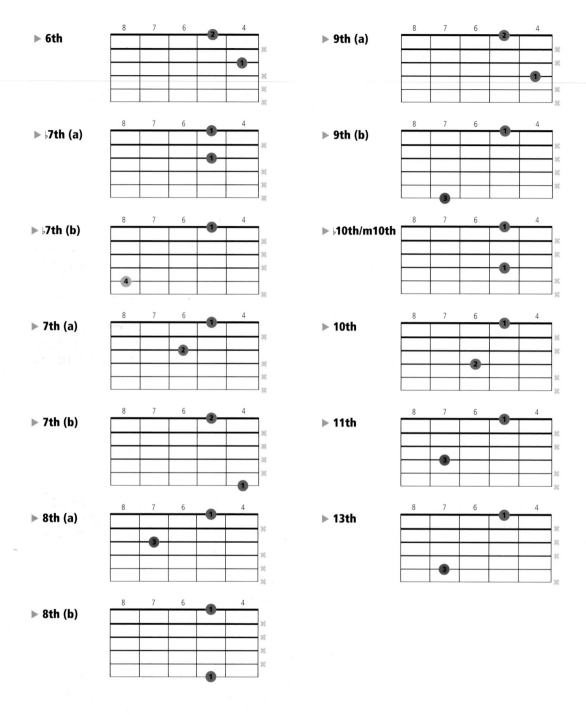

▶ **6th**

▶ **♭7th (a)**

▶ **♭7th (b)**

▶ **7th (a)**

▶ **7th (b)**

▶ **8th (a)**

▶ **8th (b)**

▶ **9th (a)**

▶ **9th (b)**

▶ **♭10th/m10th**

▶ **10th**

▶ **11th**

▶ **13th**

Basic principles of CHORD BUILDING

There are two golden rules about chromatic note relativity that you must learn if you want to use the theories set out in this chapter to be able to build chords on your guitar. It is important to be able to build chord shapes from chord names as you would see on a timing chart.

▲ **A minor**

GOLDEN RULE 1

The 3rd note always determines the major or minor status of a chord. If you play a chord containing a minor 3rd, the chord is minor. If you play a chord containing a major 3rd the chord is major. Minor and major 10th notes are the octaves (and so the same notes) of the minor and major 3rd and so the same rule applies. There are no exceptions to this rule.

If the chord you are playing says minor in its name, play a minor 3rd; if it says 'maj' or major, or indeed says nothing, play a major 3rd. The general rule is always assume you need a major 3rd unless the chord name states minor. Some examples:

An Am chord has a minor 3rd.
An A chord has a major 3rd.
An Amaj7 chord has a major 3rd.

▲ **A7**

GOLDEN RULE 2

The 7th note cannot determine the major or minor status of a chord, even though it is referred to as 'minor 7' or 'major 7'. The 7th note merely reacts to the 3rd note and has no bearing on whether a chord is major or minor. The general rule of thumb with the 7th note when building chords is always to use the dominant 7th unless the chord name states major. Some examples:

An A7 chord has a major 3rd and a dominant 7th.
An Am7 chord has a minor 3rd and a dominant 7th.
An Amaj7 chord has a major 3rd and a major 7th.

CHORD MAKE-UP

Chords are generally made up of three or four different notes, bunched together and played at the same time. Basic major and minor chords only contain three different notes and so are known as triads. A triad is made up of the 1st (root), 3rd and 5th notes of the scale. Look back at any major or minor chord in Lesson 3 (pages 26–41) to see that they only ever contain three different notes. (The same notes can be repeated at different pitches in one chord but there are only three in total.) Remember the golden rules: the 3rd dictates whether the chord is major or minor and the 7th reacts to this. In Amaj7 in the chart below, for example, see how the 7th has to be major because the chord name says so, whereas in the A7 chord, the ♭7th is used because the chord name makes no distinction between major or minor.

BASIC CHORDS IN THE KEY OF A, WITH INTERVAL NUMBERS		
CHORD NAME	INTERVAL/RELATIVE NUMBERS	CHORD MAKE-UP
A	1st, 3rd, 5th	A, C#, E
Am	1st, ♭3rd, 5th	A, C, E
A7	1st, 3rd, 5th, ♭7th	A, C#, E, G
Am7	1st, ♭3rd, 5th, ♭7th	A, C, E, G
Amaj7	1st, 3rd, 5th, 7th	A, C#, E, G#

SIXTH CHORDS

We need to look at one more type of chord to complete our study – sixth chords. There are three main types: dominant, major and minor. The following chart shows all three variants and the note intervals they are built from. Look at the difference in their make-up:

The dominant

This is the most basic sixth chord. As the chord name only says 6, there is no need to go beyond this note, but if we were to add a 7th it would have to be the dominant 7th note (G in the key of A).

The minor sixth

Again relatively straightforward, here we just flatten the 3rd to make the chord minor. If we were to extend the chord to a 7th we would use the dominant 7th note (G). Don't be confused by the name: there is no minor 6th (♭6th) interval in the chord. The 6th note is major, not flattened.

The major sixth

Here, we need to add the 7th note in order to differentiate it from the dominant sixth chord. The major 3rd isn't enough to suggest major because it also appears in the dominant sixth chord.

SIXTH CHORDS IN THE KEY OF A, WITH INTERVAL NUMBERS		
CHORD NAME	INTERVAL/RELATIVE NUMBERS	CHORD MAKE-UP
A6 (dominant)	1st, 3rd, 5th, 6th	A, C#, E, F#
Am6	1st, ♭3rd, 5th, 6th	A, C, E, F#
Amaj6	1st, 3rd, 5th, 6th, 7th	A, C#, E, F#, G#

Basic ARPEGGIOS and INVERSIONS

Pick out the notes from any chord in order and you play an arpeggio. An understanding of arpeggios is essential when writing or improvising solos to songs, since they instantly give you all the available notes in a chord. This is an excellent way of guaranteeing that you won't hit any bum notes when creating a solo.

ARPEGGIO PRACTICE
Learn the arpeggios for the eight basic chord shapes set out below and build them into each practice session. Play each arpeggio in the format 1st, 3rd, 5th, 7th and so on, ascending upward, and then reverse the pattern to return to the root note. Don't move on until you are happy with each one and have memorized the finger pattern and name.

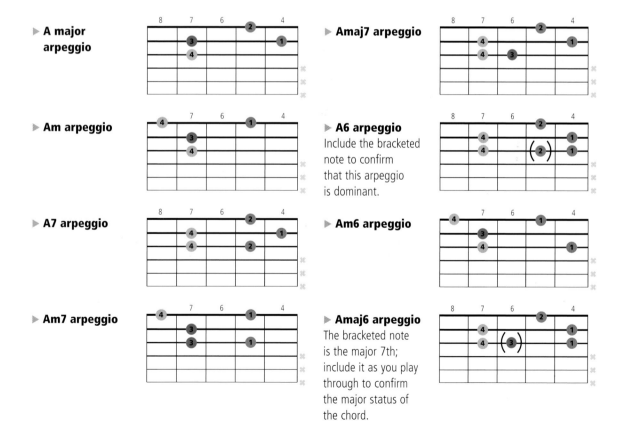

▶ **A major arpeggio**

▶ **Am arpeggio**

▶ **A7 arpeggio**

▶ **Am7 arpeggio**

▶ **Amaj7 arpeggio**

▶ **A6 arpeggio**
Include the bracketed note to confirm that this arpeggio is dominant.

▶ **Am6 arpeggio**

▶ **Amaj6 arpeggio**
The bracketed note is the major 7th; include it as you play through to confirm the major status of the chord.

INVERTING THE ORDER

If you change the order of the pattern, the resulting chord or *arpeggio* is called an *inversion*. Instead of playing a major arpeggio in the order 1st, 3rd, 5th, 8th, try playing it 3rd, 5th, 8th, 3rd. Still a major arpeggio, this version is called the first inversion. Play the same notes in the order 5th, 8th, 3rd, 5th and you have the second inversion. The notes remain the same, just played in a different order.

Arpeggio exercise 1

1 Play the major arpeggio or chord make-up in the key of A: A, C#, E, A.

2 Play the first inversion: C#, E, A, C#.

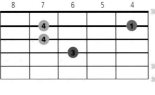

3 Now try the second inversion: E, A, C#, E.

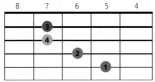

Arpeggio exercise 2

1 Where there are more notes, there can be more inversions. Try an Am7 chord: play the notes A, C, E, G, A.

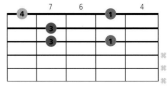

2 Play the first inversion: C, E, G, A, C.

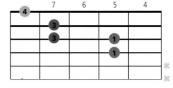

3 Now try the second inversion: E, G, A, C, E.

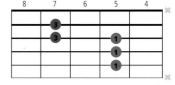

4 This time add a third inversion: G, A, C, E, G.

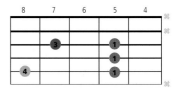

TOP TIP

Inversions add interest to any chord pattern because the displacement of the root allows other notes in the chord to increase in importance. This works especially well when playing with another musician. When you are next jamming with a friend, rather than both playing the same chord shapes, one of you should try inverting the chords to alter the sound.

JARGON BUSTER

Arpeggio Playing the composite notes of a chord individually in order.

Inversion Changing the order of the composite notes of an arpeggio.

SLASH chords

Displacing the root note in a chord or arpeggio is often used when playing in a band. When more than one instrument is performing roughly the same role inversions can help prevent sound clashes. These chords are called slash chords because of how they are written – with a slash in the middle to distinguish between the chord and the root. A/C#, for example, is an A major chord played with a C# root (the first inversion of A major). A/E is an A chord with an E root (the second inversion of A).

Playing slash chords

◀ **1** Have a go at the chord A/C#, the first inversion of A.

◀ **2** Now try the second inversion of A, A/E. Play the root note as the open 6th string so the chord has a fuller sound.

Transposing shapes exercise

◀ **1** Try two inversions in the key of C to see the shapes higher up the fingerboard. Start by playing the chord C/E, the first inversion of C.

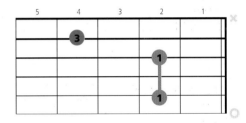

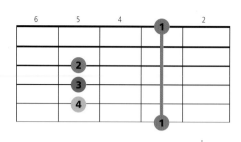

◀ **2** Move to C/G, the second inversion of C. Notice how the root is on the 6th string. Now you can use any of these shapes over a standard major chord in the key of A or C while a friend plays the standard major chord. Hear how interesting the sound is.

Exercise with other chords

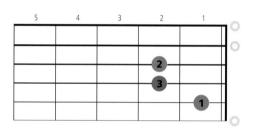

◀ **1** Let's apply the theory to other chords. Take Am and play it as a first inversion: Am/C. C is the relative major of Am, so this chord is often called Cmaj6.

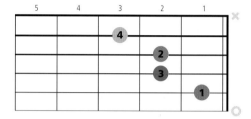

◀ **2** Move to the second inversion: Am/E.

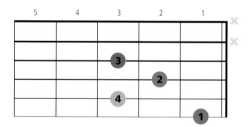

◀ **3** Look now at how the principle applies in other keys, by playing the first inversion of Dm: Dm/F. Again, this could be called Fmaj6.

◀ 4 Now play the second inversion: Dm/A.

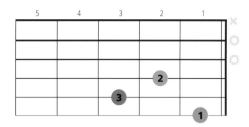

OTHER USES FOR SLASH CHORDS

Don't feel restricted to forming slash chords from chord inversions. You can work with any chord with any root note: just remember that the chord name comes before the slash and the bass note after it. All you have to do is find the chord shape, then put the bass note in as the lowest note in the chord. The bass note is usually within easy reach, so experiment with shapes until you find one that works.

Experimenting exercise

Try working out shapes for these chords: C/D, B♭m/F, Gm/D, A7/E, Fmaj7/C.

TOP TIP

When you are playing with a bass guitarist, remember that he or she plays the bass note, so you don't have to. Play instead the first part of the slash chord. When playing with another guitarist or keyboard player, consider playing both parts of the slash chord to add diversity to the sound. Using slash chords when playing solo is acceptable, but these chords can sound a little unbalanced since the root is not where it is supposed to be. And if no other instrument plays the root the effect can feel slightly empty.

LESSON SUMMARY

This chapter is a resource to dip into while you work through the other lessons in the book. Return to the basics of music theory here every week to back up the practical work you put in with the instrument on your knee. The information will inform and transform every element of your playing.

LESSON 5 BARRE CHORDS

TO BE ABLE TO SUCCESSFULLY
FRET A BARRE WITH THE FIRST FINGER
AND PLAY ALL THE BASIC BARRE
CHORD SHAPES. ALSO TO UNDERSTAND
BARRE CHORD THEORY.

To play a barre chord you lie your first finger across all the strings, in effect, replacing the nut. This takes dedication, as fretting barre chords is physically demanding, but the technique instantly increases your chord vocabulary beyond measure.

BASIC barre chords

Before learning about barre chords, most guitarists avoid playing sharp and flat chords. When F#m7 comes up in a song book, for example, the page is quickly turned. F#m7 is not a difficult chord. Nor is D♭maj7 or A♭m, but they sound difficult. Before wading in it's a good idea to build up strength in your first finger, ready for the job barre chords require of it. Introduce these exercises into your daily practice routine and work through them diligently.

ESSENTIAL EXERCISES

These exercises increase and decrease stress on your first finger gradually, helping build up strength and fluency in movement. Practise them daily until you feel confident and can hear every note clearly. Your first finger will soon be ready to attempt barre chords.

First finger exercise 1

1 Starting at the 1st fret, lie your first finger over the 1st and 2nd strings. Play these two notes, ensuring each is clear.

2 Move to the 2nd fret and cover the 1st, 2nd and 3rd strings with your first finger. Play, ensuring each note rings clearly.

3 Move your first finger to the 3rd fret, cover the bottom four strings and play them. Play the 4th fret with your first finger covering the bottom five strings. At the 5th fret, cover all six strings and strum through slowly to check that all the notes are clear. If they are not, move your first finger position within the fret and try again.

4 Continue up the neck to the 6th fret, covering only five strings. At the 7th fret cover only the four bottom strings. Move to the 8th fret and play the three bottom strings with your first finger. Finally, at the 9th fret, go back to covering just the bottom two strings.

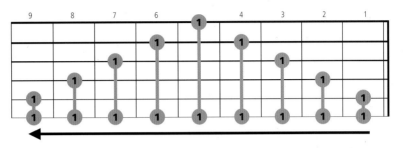

First finger exercise 2

1 Cover the five bottom strings at the 10th fret with your first finger. Adjust the position of your left hand until all the strings ring clearly.

2 Move down to the 9th fret, cover all six strings with your first finger and play through them, again making sure all the notes are clear.

3 Continue down the neck, covering five and six strings in the same manner until you reach the first fret, covering all six strings with your first finger.

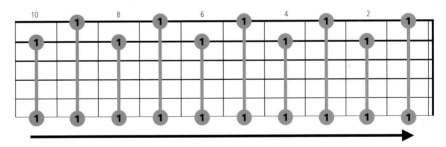

TOP TIPS

- Stop if your hand hurts. Repetitive Strain Injury is a common side effect of over-stressing the hand and must be avoided. Do a little practice often, rather than a lot of practice infrequently. Daily consistency is paramount.

- Keep your first finger as flat as you can with your thumb pressing the back of the neck in a vice-like grip. Try rolling your finger back slightly to overcome the dents in your first finger caused by the underside of your knuckles.

E-SHAPED barre chords

The E-shaped barre chord is a must for guitarists. It is easy to move around the neck and makes for simple changes of chord type. There are two main barre chord shapes to study in Lesson 5 – E- and A-shaped – and both derive from basic chord shapes that you learnt in Lesson 3 (see pages 26–41). We will look at five variants of each shape to coincide with the basic shapes you already know. Let's start with the E shape, which doesn't strain the fingers as much as the A shape.

EXERCISE: BEGINNING E-SHAPED BARRE CHORDS

◄ 1 Play an E chord in the open position as normal, but adjust your fingers so you are using your second, third and fourth fingers to fret the notes.

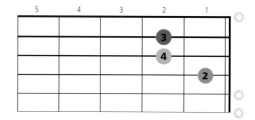

◄ 2 Slide the shape up the neck so your second finger is in the 4th fret and your third and fourth fingers are in the 5th fret.

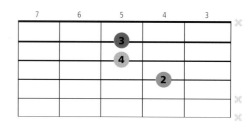

◄ 3 Lay your first finger all the way across the 3rd fret, making sure you cover all the strings evenly: there should be no nasty buzzes when you strum the chord. You have made G major barre chord at the 3rd fret using an E-shaped chord. Practise the shape in several positions around the neck. When you feel confident, move on to the next exercise.

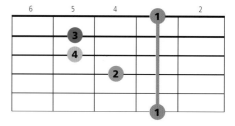

MORE BASIC CHORD SHAPES

Here are four more basic chord shapes to increase your repertoire dramatically. All the shapes are transpositional, which means they can be moved around the neck to give lots more chords without having to learn many new finger patterns.

◄ Em becomes Gm
Play an E minor chord using your third and fourth fingers, and slide them up to the 5th fret. Barre the chord off with your first finger to produce a G minor chord.

◄ E7 becomes G7
Make the E7 shape using your second and third fingers. Move it up so your second finger is in the 4th fret. Barre off the chord on the 3rd fret using your first finger to produce G7.

◄ Em7 becomes Gm7
Make the Em7 shape using your third finger on the 5th fret. Barre off the chord on the 3rd fret using your index finger to produce Gm7.

◄ Emaj7 becomes Gmaj7
Play Emaj7 on the 4th and 5th frets with your second, third and fourth fingers. Barre the 3rd fret with your first finger to produce Gmaj7.

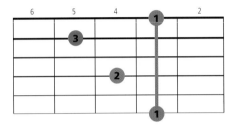

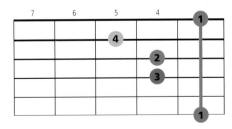

TAKING IT FURTHER

Now you've tried these barre chords on the 3rd (G) fret, why not try them on other frets? An E shape barred off on the 1st fret gives you F major. Barring it off on the 5th fret would give you A major, and so on.

A-SHAPED barre chords

The other most often-used barre chord shape is the A shape, based around the basic fingering of the open A chord and all its variants which we looked at in Lesson 4 (pages 58–60). As with the E-shaped barre chord we will learn five variants of the A shape. These are slightly more demanding on the left hand due to the positioning of the fingers, but with careful practice they are easily achievable.

EXERCISE: BEGINNING A-SHAPED BARRE CHORDS

◀ **1** Play an A chord in the open position as normal, but adjust your fingers so that you are using your second, third and fourth fingers to fret the notes instead of your first, second and third.

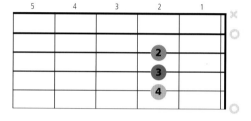

◀ **2** Slide this shape up the neck so your fingers are in the 5th fret.

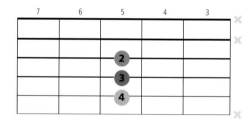

◀ **3** Lay your first finger all the way across the 3rd fret, making sure you cover every string evenly so that there are no nasty buzzes when you strum the chord. Notice that you only need to strum the bottom five strings. You have made a C major barre chord at the 3rd fret using an A-shaped chord. Practise the shape in several positions around the neck.

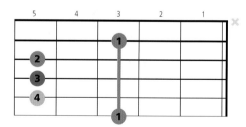

MORE BASIC CHORD SHAPES

Below are four more basic A chord shapes that will dramatically increase your barre chord repertoire.

◀ Am becomes Cm

Play an A minor chord using your second, third and fourth fingers and slide them up so the second finger is in the 4th fret. Barre the chord off with your first finger to give a C minor barre chord.

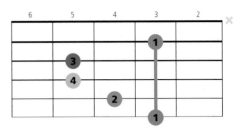

◀ A7 becomes C7

Make the A7 shape using your third and fourth fingers and move it up so that your fingers are in the 5th fret. Barre off the chord on the 3rd fret using your first finger and you now have C7.

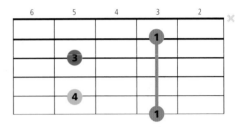

◀ Am7 becomes Cm7

Play Am7 with your second finger on the 4th fret. Barre off on the 3rd fret with your index finger to produce Cm7.

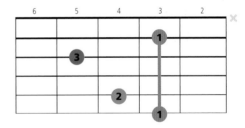

◀ Amaj7 becomes Cmaj7

Play Amaj7 with your second finger in the 4th fret and your third and fourth fingers in the 5th fret and barre the 3rd fret with your first finger. This gives you Cmaj7.

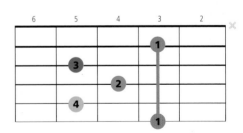

TAKING IT FURTHER

These shapes are again transpositional and so can be moved around the neck to give lots more chords. When you are confident with these shapes at the 3rd (C) fret, try moving them around the fingerboard. An A shape barred off on the 7th fret gives E major. Barred off on the 4th fret it becomes C# major, and so on.

LOCATING barre chords

Understanding and being able to play the shapes of the barre chords is only half the subject. The other half is knowing where to find them on the fingerboard and being able to get to the right chord shape in the right place quickly so that there is no stutter between chords.

EASY BARRE CHORD LOCATOR
This easy-to-follow chart helps you to locate every barre-chord position for E, A, C, G and D shape chords. O refers to the chord name as it would be played in the open position.

EASY BARRE CHORD LOCATOR

FRETS BEING BARRED

	12th	11th	10th	9th	8th	7th	6th	5th	4th	3rd	2nd	1st	O
E shape	E	D#/E♭	D	C#/D♭	C	B	A#/B♭	A	G#/A♭	G	F#/G♭	F	E
A shape	A	G#/A♭	G	F#/G♭	F	E	D#/E♭	D	C#/D♭	C	B	A#/B♭	A
C shape	C	B	A#/B♭	A	G#/A♭	G	F#/G♭	F	E	D#/E♭	D	C#/D♭	C
G shape	G	F#/G♭	F	E	D#/E♭	D	C#/D♭	C	B	A#/B♭	A	G#/A♭	G
D shape	D	C#/D♭	C	B	A#/B♭	A	G#/A♭	G	F#/G♭	F	E	D#/E♭	D

WHERE DO I PLAY THEM?
As you should by now have noticed, the two main barre chord shapes are E and A. These shapes are found in two completely different places on the neck of the guitar. For instance, a G chord as an E-shaped chord is found at the 3rd fret, while the same chord as an A shape is played at the 10th fret. It's normal to feel unsure about which shape to choose when playing barre chords, but the general rule is to stay as close to the nut as possible. It's easier to fret chords at this end of the fingerboard where the frets are slightly wider, and they tend to sound fuller than chords played higher up the neck. Of course, the decision where to play chords is ultimately up to you. The song also dictates where chords should be fretted and whether chords are sounded high or low.

CYCLE OF NOTES

As we saw in Lesson 4 (see page 43), the cycle of notes is a useful way of remembering all the notes on your guitar in order. For barre chords, it is vital that you learn all the names of the notes on the top two strings (E and A strings) that form the root notes of the two barre-chord shapes we are looking at. Below are the notes on these two strings in order, starting from the open position.

Learning E-string notes

Memorize this set of notes. See how any E-shaped barre chord played at the 8th fret has a C root and therefore is a C chord. The type of chord depends on which shape you are fingering. Try an Em-shaped chord at the 8th fret and see how to get a Cm chord.

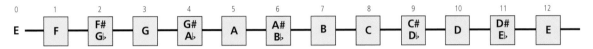

Learning A-string notes

Next memorize this run of notes. Notice how any A-shaped barre chord played at the 5th fret has a D root and so is a D chord. The type of chord again depends on which shape you are fingering, so an Am7 chord fretted at the 5th fret gives a Dm7 chord.

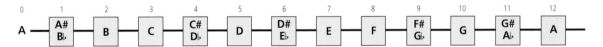

TOP TIP

Consider all options when deciding which barre chord to use. Although it is common to stay as close to the nut as possible, you may find this rule doesn't work every time. Keep an open mind and most of all make sure the chord you choose enhances the piece of music you are playing.

CHANGING barre chords

The biggest difficulty with barre chords is changing from one shape to another and from one neck position to another. It is important to change smoothly and fluently so each chord moulds gently into the next. The following exercises should help. The first chord-changing exercise helps your fingers get used to the basic change between E- and A-shaped major barre chords. The second speeds up your changes and increases familiarity with the chords.

TOP TIP

Try to find links between shapes to help you change smoothly from one to another. Leaving one finger on during a chord change, for example, can speed things up no end, so look for all possible similarities between chords.

CHANGING CHORD EXERCISE 1

1 Play an E-shaped major barre chord at the 3rd fret; this gives you a G chord.

2 Change finger position to play an A-shaped barre chord at the 3rd fret, which produces the chord C.

3 Move this finger position up one fret to the 4th fret to play a C# chord.

4 Change finger position to an E-shaped barre chord at the 4th fret, giving you G#.

5 Continue up the neck, playing an E-shaped barre chord followed by A-shaped barre chord and vice versa until you reach the 10th fret where the E-shaped chord is D and the A-shaped chord is G.

CHANGING CHORD EXERCISE 2

1 Repeat the steps from exercise 1, this time playing minor-shaped barre chords. Again start on G at the 3rd fret and work your way up the neck to the 10th fret, changing from E-shaped to A-shaped, and then A-shaped back to E-shaped.

2 Do the same using dominant seventh-shaped chords.

3 Now repeat with minor seventh-shaped chords.

4 Finally repeat the exercise using major seventh-shaped chords.

PROGRESSION EXERCISE 1

Play both the following progression sequences using barre chords. The chords in bold are E-shaped, the others A-shaped. Try to maintain the momentum of the tune while you change chord. Only strum the bottom five strings when playing any A-shaped barre chord (the 6th string will not always be in tune if you strike it by mistake).

Sequence 1

||: G / / / | C / / / | Am / / / | D / / / :||

Sequence 2

||: Bm / / / | D / / / | A / / / | F#m / / / :||

PROGRESSION EXERCISE 2

Let's make the progressions slightly more difficult by adding in some dominant seventh and minor seventh chords. Remember to keep your barre finger laid flat so all the notes ring out clearly. Only speed up when you are familiar with the shapes and chord patterns.

Sequence 1

||: B♭ / / / | Gm / / / | E♭ / / / | F / / / |
| B♭ / / / | Gm7 / / / | E♭ / / / | F7 / / / :||

Sequence 2

	: E / / /	C#m / / /	D / / /	A / / /
E / / /	C#m7 / / /	D / / /	A7 / / /
G#m7 / / /	C#m7 / / /	F#m7 / / /	B7 / / / :	

PROGRESSION EXERCISE 3

These progressions use all five barre chord shapes including the major seventh. Make sure that there are no buzzing strings: don't move on to this exercise until you can play all the chords confidently, correctly and fluently.

Sequence 1

	: Fmaj7 / / /	Dm7 / / /	B♭ / / /	C / / /
Fmaj7 / / /	Dm / / /	B♭ / / /	Am7 / / /
Dm / / /	Am / / /	B♭ / / /	C7 / / / :	

Sequence 2

	: A♭m / / /	D♭m7 / / /	A♭m / / /	A♭7 / / /
D♭m7 / / /	D♭m / / /	A♭m7 / / /	A♭7 / / /
E♭m / / /	D♭m7 / / /	A♭m / / /	E♭m7 / / / :	

OTHER barre chord shapes

Although the E- and A-shaped barre chords are the most commonly used, you can play other open-shaped chords to form barre chords. Any open chord that uses three fingers or less can, in theory, be used to form a barre chord. Experimentation is the key to success. Some of these shapes can be quite difficult to fret while your first finger forms the barre, but persevere with them as they offer different sound variations to the basic E- and A-shaped barre chords and add colour to a song or progression.

D-SHAPED BARRE CHORDS

The D chord is an obvious choice for barring because its root note falls on an open string (D string), but as you should only strum four strings when playing a barre chord, it is not particularly full sounding. The other thing to note about D-shaped barre chords is that the first finger only covers the D string and does not really form a barre. All basic D chords can be played as barre chords and moved up the fingerboard freely. You wouldn't usually employ them to play a chord progression, more to enhance one – these shapes work well as an accompaniment when another musician plays the basic chord progression.

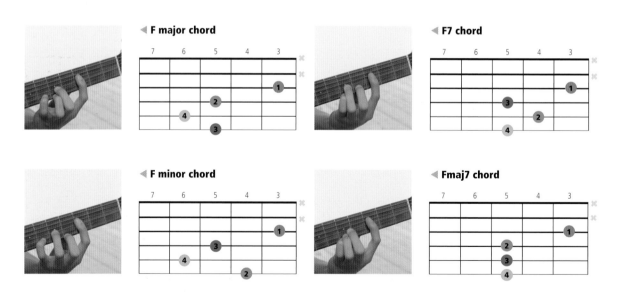

◄ **F major chord**

◄ **F7 chord**

◄ **F minor chord**

◄ **Fmaj7 chord**

C-SHAPED BARRE CHORDS

Two C chords can be turned into barre chord shapes, because both C major and Cmaj7 feature three fingers or less and open strings in their basic versions. The major seventh chord in this shape has a particularly nice sound, although it is not the most comfortable shape to play. Try the chords out now. Remember that the root note is on the A string and therefore you should not play the E string.

◀ **D major chord**

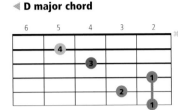

◀ **Dmaj7 chord**

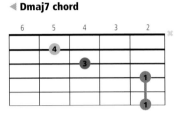

G-SHAPED BARRE CHORDS

Three G chords are eligible to become barre chord shapes. G major, G7 and Gmaj7 all fit the bill, although they are quite a stretch when played this way. G7 and Gmaj7 are especially difficult because the fourth finger has to fret the 6th string while the second finger remains on the 1st string.

Try them now. You may find it easier to roll the first finger slightly on to its side so that you are positioned with the second, third and fourth fingers ready to spread out to form the other part of the barre chord. Experiment with how many strings you lay the first finger across: you may find it easier to cover more strings than necessary.

◀ **A major chord**

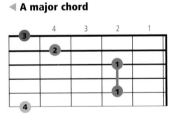

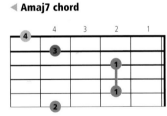

◀ **Amaj7 chord**

◀ **A7 chord**

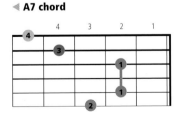

TOP TIPS

- Keep all fingers as close to the fret wires as possible.

- Don't grip too tightly with your thumb or first finger.

- Keep your first finger vertical to the fret wire. Try rolling your first finger on to its side slightly, to avoid the creases under the knuckles.

POWER chords

Often found in modern music, power chords form a fundamental part of most guitarists' chord vocabulary. They offer a way of playing one shape to cover most chordal situations. They have no definitive 3rd note and so are neither major nor minor. As a result they sound good when played using *overdrive* or *distortion*, from which they derive their name: they work well when a powerful sound is needed.

WHAT ARE POWER CHORDS?

In a power chord you dispense with the 3rd note, leaving just the 1st and 5th notes, so the sound is very sparse. The correct name for power chords is fifth chords – the only note present other than the root. The absence of the 3rd note has a massive impact on the use of the chord, because it can basically be used anywhere and therefore becomes a favourite of guitarists who can't be bothered to get to grips with barre chords. The reason these chords work so well with overdrive and distortion effects on an electric guitar is that the 3rd note often makes a chord sound muddy or discordant when played using these effects. By removing this note, chords sound great through overdrive or distortion pedals.

BASIC POWER CHORD SHAPES

◄ E-shaped power chord
Play it now and notice how the shape is the same as the bottom three notes of an E major or E minor barre chord.

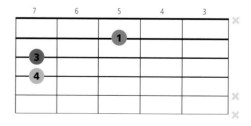

◄ A-shaped power chord
By playing it see how this chord is the same as the bottom three notes of the A major or A minor chord.

◀ D-shaped power chord
This is a slightly more difficult shape because the fourth finger has to move into the next fret up, which is a bit of a stretch. Try it now.

8	7	6	5	4
			①	
	③			
④				

JARGON BUSTER

Overdrive Term originally derived from the sound of turning up the volume of an amplifier too far, to create a crunchy tone. Today, the sound can be achieved using foot pedals (see pages 130–31).

Distortion A more extreme version of overdrive, in which the sound is distorted to create a screaming, fuzzy tone. Both effects are commonly used in heavy rock.

WHEN TO USE THEM

Power chords can be used to substitute all the barre chords you have studied. If you are playing a song that needs a distortion effect, it is almost essential to use power chords, since barre chords can sound discordant with the fuzzy tone of the effect. If you are not using an overdrive effect, always opt for barre chords. Many guitarists habitually use power chords all the time, an approach that loses the distinction of individual chord types. Power chords can sound uninteresting because they don't contain as many notes as standard barre chords. Don't give up the fuller, more rounded tone of barre chords lightly in favour of a less dynamic impostor.

LESSON SUMMARY

Your first finger should by now feel comfortable barring strings to create barre chords, and you have practised the technique until each note rings out clearly. You also understand the theory behind their make-up and use. You have seen how easy it is to fret commonly avoided 'difficult' chords, and by learning a few simple finger shapes you can now add around 120 new chords to your repertoire, many of which are sharps and flats that have seemed impossible up to now.

LESSON 6 SCALES MADE EASY

AIM TO BE ABLE TO PLAY AND USE BASIC SCALES AND TO UNDERSTAND HOW THEY CAN BE MOVED AROUND THE FINGERBOARD.

The word scale comes from the Italian *scala*, meaning stairway. Think of a scale as a ladder made up of a series of related notes, or rungs. In this lesson we look first at the most often-used scales and move progressively steadily to more difficult scales.

What are SCALES?

Each scale follows a set pattern of intervals (see Lesson 4, pages 53–55) played in a certain order. These intervals define the type of scale and its name. The key of the scale is set by the 1st, or root, note of the scale. To play scales musicians usually start at the root note, play up through one, two or three octaves to the relevant higher octave of the root note, and then play back down the pattern to the 1st note again (without stopping at the highest note).

HOW MANY SCALES ARE THERE?

There are literally hundreds of scales, with many different ways of playing each one! All we can do here is study the main scales: those you will find most useful. Learn one or two at a time and practise each so thoroughly that you understand it inside out before moving on.

WHY DO I NEED TO LEARN THEM?

Learning scale patterns and practising them regularly are the most important things you can do to help you become a 'lead' guitarist. When used correctly, scales provide all manner of notes you can use to improvise a solo over a chord pattern. The art of making up a solo from a scale is known as improvising: most good guitarists can improvise a solo over a chord pattern on first hearing it.

WHAT IS ALTERNATE PICKING?

This is the art of being able to pick fluently with the right hand using alternate down and up strokes while moving through the scale with the left hand. This is the most effective way of picking: every time the plectrum goes down it has to come

TOP TIP

Read the scale diagrams by starting at the lowest note on the 6th or 5th string (depending on the root of the scale), working up to the highest note on the 1st string, and back down to the lowest note again. Remember to play the top note only once.

back up before it can go down again. You should only pick once for each note of the scale. Practise by playing each scale three times: firstly all down strokes, secondly all up strokes, thirdly alternating down and up strokes, at first saying out loud which stroke you are executing (up or down) to help you spot mistakes. You may feel a bit silly, but it works.

FINGERING

The finger positions suggested for each scale are only a guide, but it is best to try to stick to them because they offer the most economical way of playing the scales. If you find a way that suits you better, go with it. Do, however, persevere with using all four fingers in the left hand. Failure to do this will keep your little finger weaker, which hinders progression.

PENTATONIC and BLUES scales

These are perhaps the most commonly used scales you will come across. They are very versatile and can be used over many different styles of music. You may have heard these scales being used by some of your favourite guitarists.

JARGON BUSTER

Discord The unpleasant sound produced when two or more notes clash with one another.

PENTATONIC SCALES

Split the word 'pentatonic' in two to understand it better: 'pent' means five and 'tonic' means tones. This suggests each pentatonic scale has five different notes. That doesn't mean there are only five notes in the whole scale, but that there are only five notes in each octave that can be repeated to give two or three octave variants. G pentatonic minor scale, for example, contains the notes G, B♭, C, D, F, then returns to G. To understand more, practise the following two-octave 6th and 5th string root scales. Don't move on until you feel comfortable with the left-hand positions and the up and down picking.

▶ **G pentatonic minor scale**
Start with this basic but effective scale. Play it three times: once with down strokes, once with up strokes, and finally with alternating up and down strokes.

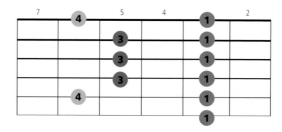

▶ **C pentatonic minor scale**
Notice the transition of the first finger on the 2nd string.

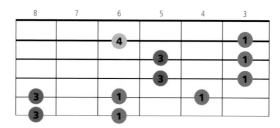

▶ **G pentatonic major scale**
Starting the scale on the second finger can seem strange. Practise so that it becomes natural.

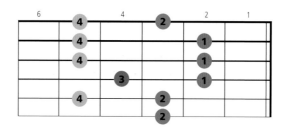

84 LESSON 6

▶ C pentatonic major scale

Make sure both notes of the transition on the G string sound clearly.

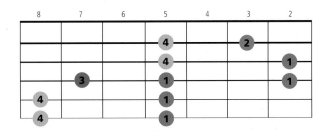

TOP TIP

You will notice with all 5th string rooted scales that there has to be a transition from one set of frets to another. If the scale starts at the 3rd fret and ends at the 8th fret, for example, you have to shift your fingers to make this possible. Make this transition as seamless as possible so the flow of the scale isn't interrupted.

Using in solos

Play pentatonic minor scale notes over minor chords in the same scale key. Play pentatonic major scale notes over major chords in the scale key.

BLUES SCALES

Almost identical to pentatonic minor scales, these are almost as commonly used. The only difference is the insertion of the 'blues' note, or ♭5th to give it its proper title. This is known as a passing note: not a note you would often stop on in the middle of a solo, since it generally produces a *discord*. Although the blues note is only one note of six, it makes such a massive difference to the sound of the scale that it becomes almost inconceivable that the pentatonic minor scale and the blues scale are so closely related. Here are two-octave blues scales to practise on the 6th and 5th string root.

▶ G blues scale

Play the scale three times, as before, noticing where the extra notes appear to make this scale differ from the pentatonic minor scale.

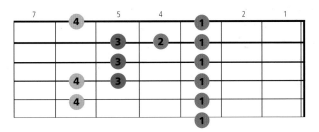

▶ C blues scale

Make sure the transition on the 2nd string is fluent and clear.

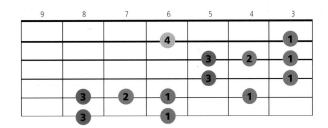

Using in solos

Try blues scales wherever you would play a pentatonic minor scale.

MAJOR and NATURAL MINOR scales

These scales relate to the diatonic note theory we looked at in Lesson 4 (see pages 53–55). They are widely used and are possibly the easiest scales to remember because, as you will hear, their note patterns sound very familiar.

MAJOR SCALES

With their distinctly happy sound, these are scales we hear all the time without realizing it, on the radio, in films, even in nursery rhymes. As the notes are very familiar, learning the major scale is made slightly easier because we can generally tell when we hit a wrong note. Practise those set out below before moving on.

▶ **G major scale 6th string root**
Notice how this scale starts on the second and fourth fingers. It is important to assign one finger per fret so your hand is evenly spread. Not starting on the first finger feels strange to begin with, but it is good practice and helps build strength in naturally weaker fingers.

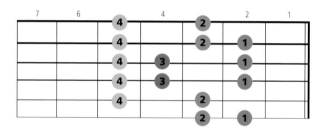

▶ **C major scale 5th string root**
Practise through the notes on the G string slowly as a separate exercise to smooth the transition on the G string. When you can play fluently, work through the whole scale.

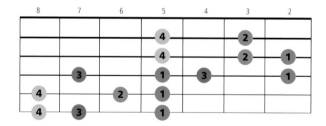

Using in solos
Major scales work best over major chords or any chord diatonically linked to the key you are in. For example, G major scale is best used over G major or any of the other six diatonic relatives in the key of G.

NATURAL MINOR SCALES

These also fit the diatonic note pattern, since they are the relative minor scales, played at the 6th degree of the major scale. In the key of G major, for instance, the natural minor scale would be played in Em, and in the key of C major it would be played in Am. Learn the natural minor scales below in their own right and don't always think of them as closely linked to the major scale.

▶ G natural minor scale 6th string root

This is a slightly awkward scale as the first finger starts in the 3rd fret, then moves back to the 2nd fret on the G string and up to the 3rd fret on the B string. This takes getting used to, so practise the transition slowly and speed up as you become more confident.

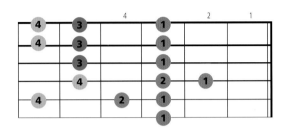

▶ C natural minor scale 5th string root

The A string root scale is much easier to learn, the only tricky transition is on the 1st string where the fourth finger has to move to the 8th fret. Make sure you pick the two notes played by the fourth finger separately: don't tie them together with a left-hand slide.

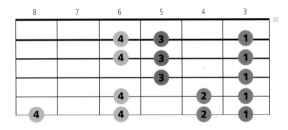

Using in solos

The natural minor scale is the fundamental minor scale, so can be used over any minor chord but it is best over the 6th degree chord shape in the diatonic note pattern, or the relative minor position. Playing the natural minor scale in G minor works best over a G minor chord, the relative minor of Bb. So any chord in the diatonic note pattern of Bb major could, in theory, be played over using the G natural minor scale. Why not try this out yourself?

HARMONIC and MELODIC MINOR scales

Although these are minor scales, both differ from the natural minor scale in the same way. They each use the major 7th note as the leading note to the 8th note. The natural minor scale uses the dominant 7th note: when you start practising you'll hear the vast difference this makes.

HARMONIC MINOR SCALES

Almost every note in this scale is identical to the natural minor scale; the exception is the 7th note, which gives the distinct and instantly recognizable sound. As you play through the following examples, hear the very definite tonal shift from the ♭6th note to the 7th.

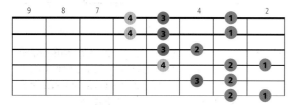

▲ G harmonic minor scale 6th string root
Get used to the shift from the fourth finger on the 5th string to the second finger on the D string. (Resist the urge to use your first finger.)

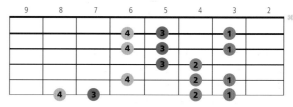

▲ C harmonic minor scale 6th string root
See how similar this scale is to the natural minor: find the one-note difference on the 3rd and 1st strings.

Using in solos
Choosing harmonic minor scales for improvising is trickier than using natural minors thanks to the 7th note. The ideal chord to use these scales over is a minor chord with a major 7th note (written as m+7). Try them also over any minor chord when a solo calls for a distinctly minor sound.

MELODIC MINOR SCALES

These are interesting scales because in their standard 'classical' format they ascend using one set of notes and descend using a completely different set. This makes them very difficult to improvise with. Most players work on an adapted version of the scale, which we will call the 'jazz' version. Practise both now.

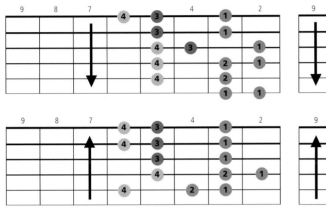

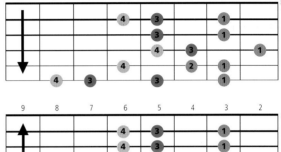

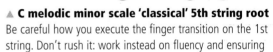

▲ G melodic minor scale 'classical' 6th string root

The main difference between this scale and the harmonic minor scale is that here the 6th note is not flattened. Notice as you play how the descending part of the scale is the same as the natural minor scale.

▲ C melodic minor scale 'classical' 5th string root

Be careful how you execute the finger transition on the 1st string. Don't rush it: work instead on fluency and ensuring that you don't slide the third or fourth fingers.

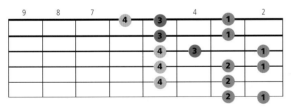

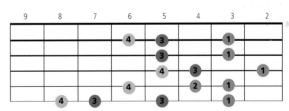

▲ G melodic minor scale 'jazz' 6th string root

As you play, notice how this scale goes up and comes down in the same way.

▲ C melodic minor scale 'jazz' 5th string root

Note the finger transition on the 1st string is the same as the transition in the classical version of the scale.

Using in solos

Jazz versions of these scales are much more useful for improvisation, since you only have to concentrate on one finger pattern.

Introducing MODES

The term 'mode' describes any scale pattern played progressively moving up the fingerboard, each mode starting on the next degree or interval of the scale. Imagine improvising over a song in the key of Gm. Having memorized the pentatonic minor and various other minor scales in the key of G minor, you should be soloing confidently. But if the key changes to Bm, many guitarists flounder. The answer is to move the G minor scales to the Bm fret (7 as E string root) so you are in the key of B minor. Once you understand modes, it really is that simple!

HOW ARE MODES FORMED?

Take a scale, break it down into the notes of its basic interval pattern and form a new scale (or mode) for each note (with new finger patterns). The notes of the G pentatonic minor scale, for instance, are G – B♭ – C – D – F. Each mode is played in order starting on these notes. If each mode were rooted on the 6th string, the first mode would start at the 3rd fret (G), the second at the 6th fret (B♭), the third at the 8th fret (C), the fourth at the 10th fret (D) and the fifth at the 13th fret (F).

PENTATONIC MODE PATTERN	
G – B♭ – C – D – F	G pentatonic minor scale
B♭ – C – D – F – G	B♭ pentatonic major scale
C – D – F – G – B♭	G pentatonic minor scale with a C root
D – F – G – B♭ – C	G pentatonic minor scale with a D root
F – G – B♭ – C – D	G pentatonic minor scale with an F root

1 Study these patterns. See how each mode starts on the second note of the preceding mode. This is because each mode starts on the next note in the scale pattern being studied. See how from the G in the top left-hand corner, the pattern is the same vertically as it is horizontally.

2 Think of modes as the first scale played each time starting on a different root note. Think also of the first mode, G minor pentatonic, as the relative minor mode of B♭ major pentatonic.

TRANSPOSITION

Like barre chords, scales can be transposed, one finger pattern used all over the fingerboard to give twelve different scales. This is very handy: you don't need to learn a different pattern for each key. All you need to know is the scale pattern you want to use and the position of the root note on the 6th or 5th string to play the scale or mode determined by the key of the piece that you are soloing over.

PENTATONIC modes

These are built from the basic pentatonic minor scale with each subsequent mode starting on the next degree of the scale. There are five modes in total as there are only five notes in the pentatonic scale. Pentatonic modes are essential learning for the guitarist because so many popular songs and guitar solos are built entirely from these scales, including much of the music we hear on television and radio. These are essential soloing tools.

HOW TO LEARN THEM

We will look at each mode in two different fingerboard positions, with a 6th string root and 5th string root. Study them in both positions to gain a solid understanding that will eventually enable you to use them to improvise in every key all over the fingerboard. None of the pentatonic modes has a particular name, so think of them as the 1st mode, but each time starting on a different root note. Essentially, all modes are one scale played all over the fingerboard starting on each of its component notes.

6TH STRING ROOT PENTATONIC MODES
(OVER TWO OCTAVES)

▶ **G pentatonic minor scale**
This should be familiar by now, but practise again using the three methods of picking, as before.

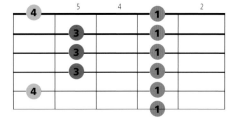

▶ **G pentatonic minor scale/B♭ root**
As you practise bear in mind that this is also known as B♭ pentatonic major scale.

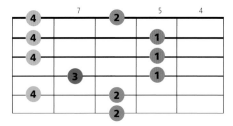

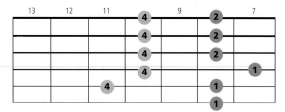

▲ G pentatonic minor scale/C root
Note the same note pattern, but starting on C.

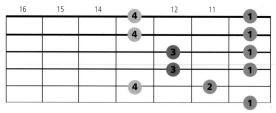

▲ G pentatonic minor scale/D root
Be sure to only use your second and fourth fingers on the B string.

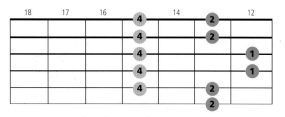

▲ G pentatonic minor scale/F root
The 2nd note of this mode is the 1st note of mode number one.

▼ Putting them into action
Play over chords in the key of G minor or B♭ major, or, as commonly used, over standard 12-bar blues progressions in the key of the 1st mode. Experiment playing one mode at a time over the following blues-based chord progression. You should be able to make all the scales work if you play them in the positions learnt above. Once you are confident in one mode, move to the next. This helps you remember the modes individually and makes it easier to use them as a group.

‖: Gm	/	/	/	Cm	/	/	/	Gm	/	/	/	Gm7	/	/	/
Cm	/	/	/	Cm7	/	/	/	Gm	/	/	/	Gm7	/	/	/
Dm7	/	/	/	Cm	/	/	/	Gm	/	/	/	Dm7	/	/	/ :‖

5TH STRING ROOT PENTATONIC MODES (OVER TWO OCTAVES)

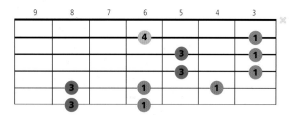

▲ C pentatonic minor scale
Play this now, using correct fingering for the transition on the 2nd string.

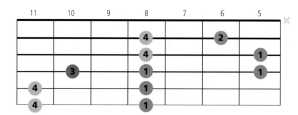

▲ C pentatonic minor scale/E♭ root
As you practise, remember this is otherwise known as E♭ pentatonic major scale.

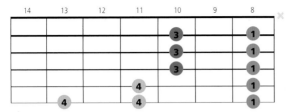

▲ **C pentatonic minor scale/F root**
Don't slide the fourth finger on the 1st string.

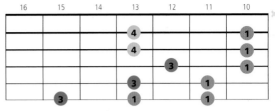

▲ **C pentatonic minor scale/G root**
Play both first finger notes clearly on the 1st string.

▲ **C pentatonic minor scale/B♭ root**
The 2nd note of this mode forms the 1st note of mode number one.

▼ **Putting them into action**
This version of the pentatonic modes sounds good over chords in the key of C minor or E♭ major. Again, they work especially well over standard 12-bar blues progressions in the key of the 1st mode. Try working at the modes using this chord progression as backing. All the modes played as written above fit well with these chords. Don't progress until you can play fluently.

```
||: Cm      /      /      /  | Fm      /      /      /  | Cm      /      /      /  | Cm7      /      /      /  |

|  Fm      /      /      /  | Fm7     /      /      /  | Cm      /      /      /  | Cm7      /      /      /  |

|  Gm7     /      /      /  | Fm      /      /      /  | Cm      /      /      /  | Gm7      /      /      /  :||
```

MOVING ON

You won't always want to play modes in the key you've learnt them here. It takes time to figure out where to play them in a different key: remember that since all the notes are repeated above the 12th fret, you can play scales lower down the fingerboard if you find yourself too far up the neck. If, for example, you were to play the 6th string root pentatonic modes starting on D at the 10th fret, you would be at fret 13 by the 2nd mode. Move it down to the 1st fret to play the same notes, but an octave lower – a handy trick that aids full use of the fingerboard.

BLUES modes

Blues modes are very similar to pentatonic modes; the difference is the addition of one 'blues' note. But what a difference this makes to the sound. The ♭5th or 'blues' note enhances any solo immeasurably. Don't overuse it when soloing, but place it thoughtfully in your lines as a 'passing note': it can sound discordant when lingered on for too long. Quick flurries of notes passing through the blues note sound great in most types of music, so when you have familiarized yourself with the modes, consider this improvisation idea. As with the pentatonic modes, blues modes don't have names, so again we will name them after the 1st mode and adjust the root note accordingly. Work through each of the modes below carefully, following all the finger directions.

6TH STRING ROOT BLUES MODES (TWO OCTAVES)

▶ **G blues scale**
This is a scale you should already know, but practise it until it becomes second-nature.

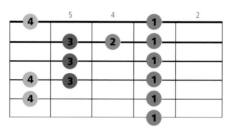

▶ **G blues scale/B♭ root**
Pick all the first finger slides clearly.

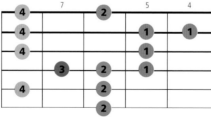

▶ **G blues scale/C root**
Notice that the first finger has to change fret on the G string. Try to do this as fluently as possible.

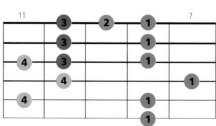

▶ G blues scale/D root

Notice that the first finger has to change fret on the B string. Try to do this as fluently as possible.

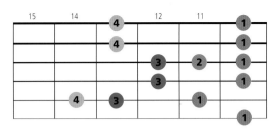

▶ G blues scale/F root

See how the fourth finger has to slide up a fret on the A string. Make sure that you pick both notes clearly.

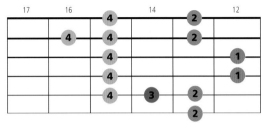

Putting them into action

Use blues modes anywhere pentatonic modes are used, over chords in G minor or B♭ major. Try this exercise over a minor 12-bar blues progression. Work on one mode at a time and move on only when you feel confident and familiar with the note pattern. These modes can be quite awkward to play, but instantly sound good when perfected.

```
||: Gm7  /   /   / | Cm7  /   /   / | Gm   /   /   / | Gm   /   /   / |
|  Cm   /   /   / | Cm   /   /   / | Gm   /   /   / | Gm   /   /   / |
|  Dm   /   /   / | Cm   /   /   / | Gm7  /   /   / | Dm7  /   /   / :||
```

5TH STRING ROOT BLUES MODES (TWO OCTAVES)

▶ C blues scale

You should be familiar with this pattern by now, but practise until it feels comfortable.

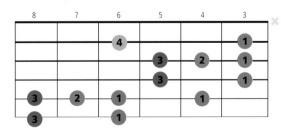

▶ C blues scale/E♭ root
Note the awkward finger transition on the 3rd string.

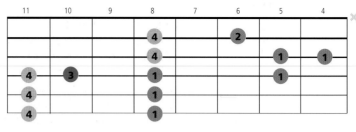

▶ C blues scale/F root
Make sure both notes played by the fourth finger are picked clearly on the 1st string; don't slide the finger up.

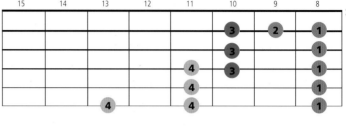

▶ C blues scale/G root
See how the first finger has to move quite a few frets in this mode.

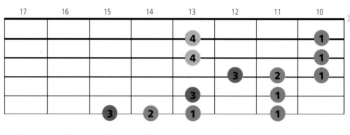

▶ C blues scale/B♭ root
The fourth finger figures heavily in this mode, so work to make all transitions smooth and clean.

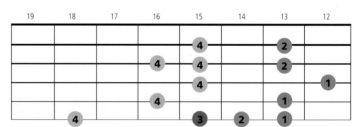

Putting them into action

These blues modes work over chords in the key of C minor or E♭ major, like the pentatonic modes. Blues modes work over most styles of music, although they are most commonly used in 'blues'. Practise them over this minor blues chord chart in C minor. Blues modes are very satisfying to play because they offer an extra element over the pentatonic modes.

```
||: Cm7  /  /  / | Fm7  /  /  / | Cm   /  /  / | Cm   /  /  / |
|  Fm   /  /  / | Fm   /  /  / | Cm   /  /  / | Cm   /  /  / |
|  Gm   /  /  / | Fm   /  /  / | Cm7  /  /  / | Gm7  /  /  / :||
```

ONE MORE MODE?

It can be argued that there should be six blues modes, since there are six notes in the blues scale. (Modes are built from each degree of the first scale position.) However, the blues note is really only a passing note and so perhaps does not warrant its own mode. If you don't think other blues modes should exist, turn the page and move on. We have learnt modes that start one note below and one note above the blues note, so we can form a mode from the ♭5th degree of the scale, as follows:

▶ G blues mode/D♭ root

Try this out and you will hear how awkward it sounds because of its first and last notes.

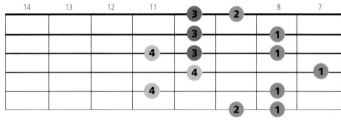

▶ C blues mode/G♭ root

It doesn't sound any better in this key.

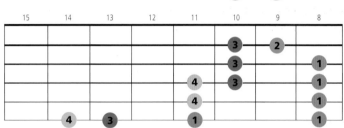

DIATONIC modes

Formed using the same theory as pentatonic and blues modes, these modes are built from the seven steps of the major scale, with each mode starting on a different degree of the scale. Each one has a name taken from Classical Greek modes. The 1st mode is named the Ionian mode and is the same as the major scale. We will study these modes in two neck positions each: the 6th and 5th string root. Pay close attention to the suggested fingerings as these are quite complex scales.

6TH STRING ROOT DIATONIC MODES (TWO OCTAVES)

▶ **G Ionian mode**
You should be familiar with this standard major scale, but practise until fluent.

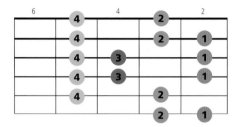

▶ **A Dorian mode**
Notice the transition of the first finger from 5th fret to 4th on the 4th and 3rd strings. Work on playing this evenly.

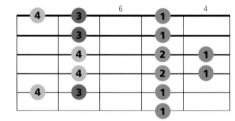

▶ **B Phrygian mode**
This scale is the first we have seen that uses the ♭2nd as the 2nd note; it is usually the standard 2nd.

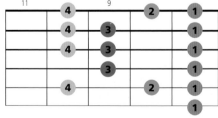

▶ **C Lydian mode**
As you practise this mode note how similar this is to the Ionian mode but using the ♭5th instead of the perfect 4th note.

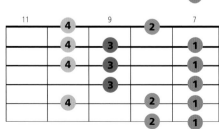

▶ D Mixolydian mode

Again, note the similarity to the Ionian mode, but using the dominant 7th note instead of the major or standard 7th.

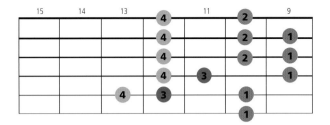

▶ E Aeolian mode

This should feel familiar; it is another name for the natural minor scale. Notice that it falls on the 6th degree of the diatonic mode pattern.

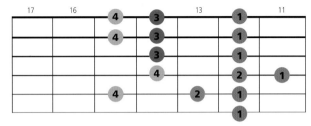

▶ F# Locrian mode

Hear the unusual sound afforded by using the ♭2nd and ♭5th notes.

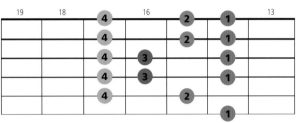

5TH STRING ROOT DIATONIC MODES (TWO OCTAVES)

▶ C Ionian mode

Practise the 1–3–1–3 finger pattern on the 3rd string slowly as this type of finger transition can prove testing.

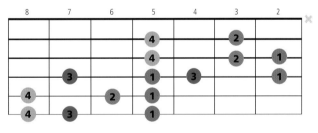

▶ D Dorian mode

Notice again how the fourth finger takes care of the two highest notes in the scale.

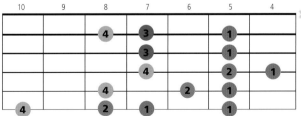

▶ E Phrygian mode
Make sure you use all four fingers as suggested to play this scale smoothly.

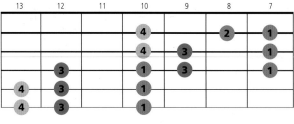

▶ F Lydian mode
Play using mainly the first, third and fourth fingers, but remember to start on the second finger.

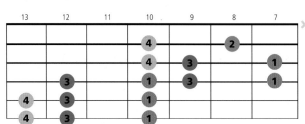

▶ G Mixolydian mode
Note how you play this scale almost entirely without using the third finger, which is quite rare.

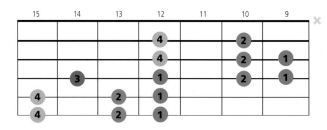

▶ A Aeolian mode
This should feel familiar; it is another name for the 5th string root natural minor scale.

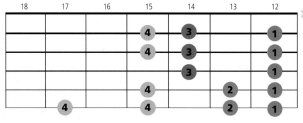

▶ B Locrian mode
Study carefully the finger transition on the 3rd string: it can easily trip you up.

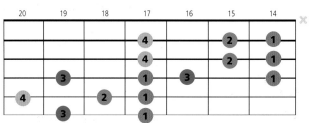

HOW DO THE MODES FIT WITH CHORDS?
Each of these modes has a chord that fits it perfectly (see chart right): the same chords studied in diatonic note relativity in Lesson 4 (see pages 53–55). When these modes are played over their relative chords they sound great, but that is not to say that they can't be used elsewhere. Again, experimentation will help you ascertain where the diatonic modes work and where they don't.

TOP TIP

Fully commit these modes to memory before trying to use them as an improvising tool. Slowly experiment with ways of using them: change the order of the notes or start in the middle of the scale, for example. It helps initially to think of the diatonic modes as seven different scales. Get to know the name of each and where it is most commonly used. As you become more familiar with the modes, you will find yourself thinking of them as one big scale played over seven fingerboard positions. But if you start out thinking of the modes in this way, invariably you get used to playing in one position only, which isn't helpful in the long term.

DIATONIC MODES AND CHORDS IN THE KEY OF G	
DIATONIC MODE	PERFECT CHORD
G Ionian mode	Gmaj7
A Dorian mode	Am7
B Phrygian mode	Bm7
C Lydian mode	Cmaj7#11
D Mixolydian mode	D7
E Aeolian mode	Em
F# Locrian mode	F#m7♭5

DIATONIC MODES AND CHORDS IN THE KEY OF C	
DIATONIC MODE	PERFECT CHORD
C Ionian mode	Cmaj7
D Dorian mode	Dm7
E Phrygian mode	Em7
F Lydian mode	Fmaj7#11
G Mixolydian mode	G7
A Aeolian mode	Am
B Locrian mode	Bm7♭5

Putting them into action

1 Play the 6th string root modes in the key of G over this chord progression. Remember all the modes work over all the chords in this progression. There is no need to change scale every time you change chord. Work on one mode at a time, concentrating on getting it to sound right before moving on to the next.

```
||: Gmaj7   /   /   / | Am7   /   /   / | Bm7   /   /   / | Em   /   /   / |
| Am7   /   /   / | Bm7   /   /   / | C   /   /   / | D7   /   /   / :||
```

2 Now improvise using the 5th string root modes over this new chord progression. Work on one mode at a time, as before.

```
||: Cmaj7   /   /   / | Dm7   /   /   / | Em7   /   /   / | Am   /   /   / |
| Dm7   /   /   / | Em7   /   /   / | F   /   /   / | G7   /   /   / :||
```

LESSON SUMMARY

Dip into this chapter weekly and with practice you will have at your fingertips the most useful scales a guitarist needs. It may take months for you to learn them all — and to be able to play them fluently. Familiarized with the scale shapes, you have had a go at improvising over chord types. It may still seem impossible to improvize a solo over a chord pattern on first hearing, but with practise it is achievable.

LESSON 7 SOLOING

AIM TO UNDERSTAND HOW TO USE
SCALES AND TECHNIQUES IN
IMPROVISATION AND TO DEVELOP AN
INDIVIDUAL STYLE AND SOUND.

Improvisation is the art of being able to create a guitar solo
without previously working anything out. A sound knowledge of
scales forms the basis of this, allowing you to build a fluent and
rounded solo over any given chord progression.

Introducing IMPROVISATION

To many players, the ability to improvise is elusive. It is possible to know hundreds of different
scales by heart, but if you don't understand the basics of improvising you may never be able
to use their notes successfully. It takes a lot of practice and a lot of wrong notes to get it
right. It is true to say you never stop learning to improvise, because there is always a new
chord chart to solo over or a different song to play.

SONGWRITING TERMS

Intro The start of a song.

Verse Main body of a song.

Chorus Catchy part that is
memorable and singalong.

Mid. or middle 8 Eight bars in
the middle of a song that are
different to the rest of the tune.

Coda The end of a song,
commonly called the outro.

HOW DO I USE SCALES AND MODES?

This is a difficult question, because improvisation isn't only about being able to
play scales well. To be able to improvise you need to know the scales you are
using so well that you can forget the mechanics of the note pattern and just let
the notes flow through your fingers. Improvisation is about being able to use the
notes from the scale to tell a musical story: to keep the listener's attention, to
build to a climax and to break off leaving the listener wanting more.

Play around with each scale as you become familiar with it and mix up the notes
so you learn them in different orders. Once you know them like the back of your
hand, experiment with them, playing them over chord patterns to find out what
works and what doesn't. The more you practise improvising, the more you will
understand where scales and modes can be used and, more importantly, where
they can't.

STEALING LICKS

It is a common misconception that you should copy the *riffs and licks* of players
you like. This is only a part truth. It is a great idea to learn riffs you love and listen
to other players – check out how they use scales and stylistic techniques. But
change the ideas before playing them in your own solos.

JARGON BUSTER

Riffs and licks Common terms used to describe the segments that make up a solo.

Add your own ideas to personalize them (and cover up the source of your inspiration) and work on building your own licks and riffs. Try not to get hung up on an individual guitarist. You will end up sounding like him or her. This might sound good now, but shows a massive lack of originality. You need to set the world on fire as a guitarist in your own right.

STRING BENDING and SLURS

String bends cause a rise or fall in the pitch of a note. Guitarists create a slur by plucking a string once with the right hand and using a movement in the left hand to set up other notes. The effect created by string bends and slurs allows fluent transition between notes.

BENDING STRINGS

This is a great-sounding technique for soloing as it smoothly moulds two notes together. There are different types of bend but all use the same basic left-hand action. Up bends are created when the tension of a guitar string is increased by pushing the string up or down with the left hand. Down bends require a pre-bend of the string before executing the bend. The fusion of the two creates a longer pitch change. In unison bends you play two notes together, bending only one.

◀ **Playing up bends**
Play the 7th fret on the G string with your third finger. Push the string upward while the note is ringing to hear the pitch of the note rising. Pull the string downward to create the same effect.

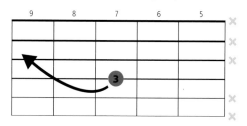

◀ **Playing down bends**
Fret the 7th fret on the G string but, before playing the note, bend the string upward. Play the note and bend the string back down again. The pitch of the note falls as the string tension decreases.

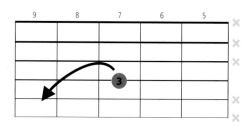

◀ **Playing up and down bends**
Play the same note as before and execute an up bend. While the note is still ringing, continue the bend back to where you started. Do not bend the note further than the note you started on.

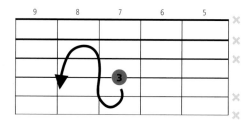

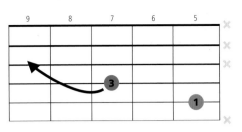

◀ **Playing unison bends**
With your third finger on the 7th fret of the G string, place your first finger on the 5th fret of the B string. Play both notes bending the note fretted with your third finger upward so its pitch is the same as the note fretted with your first finger.

TOP TIPS

• Use two or three fingers for strength when executing bends.

• Remember: you can also hammer on and pull off to and from an open string.

PLAYING SLURS

There are three main types of slur, all of which produce the same sound effect. Hammering-on creates a second note when a finger of the left hand hammers on to the fingerboard. In a pull-off, a second note is sounded by pulling the finger off the first note played. In slide technique a second note is sounded by moving the finger up a fret or two.

▶ **Playing hammer-ons**
Fret the 5th fret on the B string with your first finger. Play this note and while it is ringing hammer the third finger down on to the 7th fret of the same string.

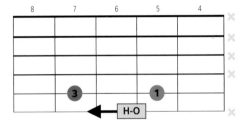

▶ **Playing pull-offs**
Fret the B string with your third finger and have the first finger ready on the 5th fret of the same string. Play the 7th fret and pull the third finger off to release the note fretted by the first finger.

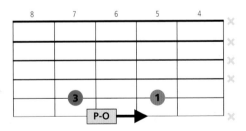

▶ **Playing slides**
Play the B string at the 5th fret with your first finger. While the note is ringing, slide the finger into the 6th fret, or even up to the 7th.

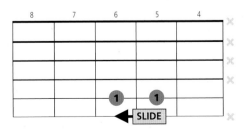

VIBRATO and HARMONICS

If you want to intensify the impact of notes, these might be your methods of choice. Vibrato is the wavering of the pitch of a note with the finger and harmonics are an interesting pitch variation created by gently touching a string.

TOP TIP

When using horizontal and wrist vibrato release the thumb from the back of the guitar neck to allow the hand to move more freely.

VIBRATO

Three main types of vibrato add a special warmth to solos. The wavering of pitch is a movement in the sound of the note that attracts the listener's attention to it.

◀ **Playing vertical vibrato**
Play any note with any finger. While the note is ringing, gently move the finger up and down in the fret, keeping the string pressed down on to the fingerboard.

Playing horizontal vibrato
Play any note again, but this time move the finger from side to side in the fret. The modulation in pitch is small, but the effect is great. This is a more classical technique.

Playing wrist vibrato
This fuses the two previous styles. Play a note, then gently move your wrist in a circular motion, effectively drawing a tiny circle on the fingerboard with the end of your finger.

HARMONICS

These are sometimes called 'artificial harmonics', although they are not an artificial sound. You can play harmonics in three ways, each giving a slightly different effect. The first method is the technique you learnt for tuning the guitar in Lesson 1 (see page 14). The second is a difficult technique that requires much practice, but the more you get used to it, the more harmonics you will begin to find all over the neck. The final technique is often used in rock solos, heard as a screaming sound from the guitar. It is very difficult to perfect but sounds great.

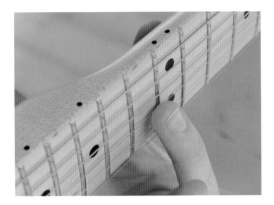

◄ **Playing harmonics 1**
Play the open G string, but lay a finger very gently over the 12th fret wire. Do not press the string down to the fingerboard. The sound you hear is a harmonic.

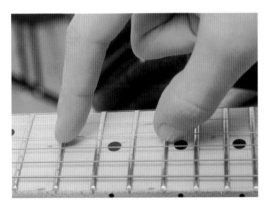

◄ **Playing harmonics 2**
Fret the 1st fret on the G string with the first finger of your left hand. With the first finger of your right hand gently touch the G string over the 13th fret wire and pick the string with your right thumb.

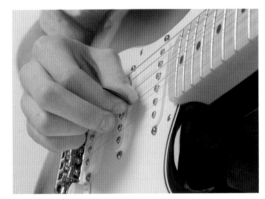

◄ **Playing harmonics 3**
Play the 7th fret on the G string. With your right hand move your thumb right to the edge of your plectrum so when you strike the note your thumb catches on the string. Move the position you strike the string with the right hand back and forth until you hear a subtle harmonic note. With overdrive or distortion (see page 131) the effect created is amazing. This is called a 'pinch harmonic'.

TOP TIP

Harmonics can be found all over the fingerboard. Experiment to see how many you can find.

FINGER tapping

There are many different ways to play fast solos, but none as visually impressive as finger tapping, where the right hand taps notes on the fingerboard as well as the left hand. This is a technique often used in rock, but it is by no means style specific; it can be used over any type of music to great effect. Use couplet tapping if the two notes being played are too far apart to reach with the left hand only. Triplet tapping creates a run of three simultaneous notes, quadruplet tapping four simultaneous notes. Have fun practising these techniques at various intervals all over the fingerboard on different strings.

TOP TIP

Why do you have to use the third finger to tap? Simple: you don't have to put down your plectrum to execute the move.

SIMPLE TAPPING EXERCISE

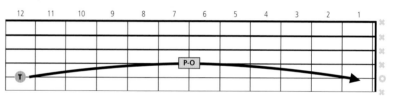

▲ Before attempting the following exercises, try tapping the second finger of your right hand on to a string at the 12th fret. Make sure the note produced rings clearly. When you are happy with this, tap the finger down again, but this time pull it off to release the open string. You should hear two clear notes. Work on this technique before moving on.

COUPLET TAPPING EXERCISE

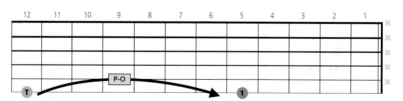

▲ Fret the 5th fret of the 1st string with the first finger of your left hand. Tap the third finger of your right hand on to the 12th fret of the 1st string and immediately pull it off to release the note fretted by the left hand. Practise at various intervals over the fingerboard on different strings.

TRIPLET TAPPING EXERCISE

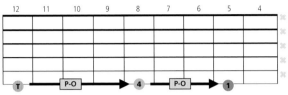

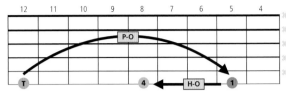

▲ 1 Using your left hand fret the 1st string 5th fret with your first finger and the 1st string 8th fret with the fourth finger. Now tap the third finger of your right hand on the 1st string 12th fret and pull it off to release the 8th fret note. Immediately pull off to release the 5th fret note. You should hear three clear notes.

▲ 2 Using the same hand positions, tap the 12th fret with the third finger of your right hand. This time pull off to the note at the 5th fret and immediately hammer your fourth finger on to the 8th fret. This creates a different sound as the pitch of the note goes down and then back up again.

QUADRUPLET TAPPING EXERCISE 1

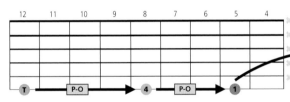

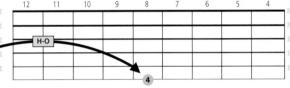

▲ 1 Using your left hand fret the 1st string 5th fret with your first finger and the 1st string 8th fret with your fourth finger. Tap your right-hand third finger on to the 12th fret, pull of to the 8th fret, then pull off to the 5th fret.

▲ 2 Lastly, hammer your fourth finger back on to the 8th fret, creating four separate notes.

QUADRUPLET TAPPING EXERCISE 2

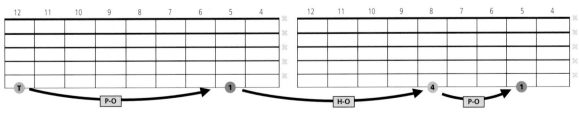

▲ 1 This time tap your right-hand third finger on to the 12th fret, pull off to the 5th fret.

▲ 2 Hammer back on to the 8th fret with your fourth finger and immediately pull off to the 5th fret, creating four separate notes.

SLIDE guitar

The art of playing slide guitar merits an entire book itself. Here we can at least study how and why it works and ways to build some of its techniques into your soloing. A slide is a cylindrical metal or glass tube that fits over a finger of the left hand. Because slides were originally made of glass, they are often called 'bottlenecks'. The advantage of a slide is that you can use it to join notes in a solo smoothly by sliding between them, providing a seamless join with none of the jumps usually produced by fret wires.

TOP TIP

Do you need a different instrument to play slide guitar? Not exactly; it depends on how seriously you intend to play. To play slide guitar successfully you need an instrument with a high action, or strings a long way from the fingerboard. This reduces the risk of hitting the fret wires when sliding. Many guitarists favour heavy-gauge strings: their higher tension makes it harder to hit fret wires by mistake. This, of course, goes against everything normally required by a guitarist: a low action and relatively light-gauge strings are generally considered an advantage.

OPEN TUNING

This is the main reason why slide guitar is a big enough subject to warrant its own book. Many slide guitarists 'open tune' their guitars, tuning strings to one chord. When the strings are strummed without frets being pressed they produce a chord. This, of course, makes it much easier to use a slide, because every fret you lay the slide over gives a barred version of a chord.

Tuning exercise

1 Tune your guitar to D – G – D – G – B – D, an open G chord.

2 Lay the slide across any fret to find a chord. In this tuning fret 1 is G#, fret 2 is A, and so on up the neck.

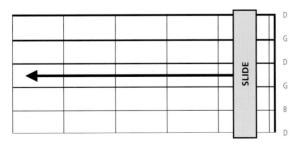

Using a slide

Most guitarists place the slide on the little finger, freeing the other three fingers to play chords and other notes. You might also like to try your third finger, which offers slightly more control. Don't press down on the fingerboard; gently lie the slide on the strings as if playing a harmonic. The effect of a slide comes from the lack of resistance moving up or down a string, unlike when moving over fret wires.

Electric guitar CONTROLS

Tremolo arms, pick-up selectors and volume and tone controls on electric guitars can be used to greatly enhance the sound of your soloing, and these controls are often overlooked as soloing tools. These four are a simple but effective way of improving your sound.

TOP TIP

The sound made by a tremolo arm is hard to mimic in any other way, so it is a useful tool. But beware if you break a string, the whole guitar goes out of tune: because the bridge isn't fixed it moves as tension decreases.

TREMOLO ARM

Often referred to as the 'whammy bar' because of the sound it produces, the correct name for this piece of kit is a tremolo arm as it produces a tremolo effect when used. When the tremolo arm was first used in the 1950s, it was to create a gentle wavering or tremolo (fluctuating pitch) effect on the notes. As time has gone on, its use has become more diverse. Many rock players use it for 'dive bombing', slackening off the string so greatly with the tremolo arm that the note disappears altogether.

▲ How does it work?
The tremolo arm is attached to the bridge. Since the bridge is usually only secured to the guitar's body at the front, when the arm is pushed toward the body or pulled away from it, the back of the bridge moves, increasing or decreasing the tension of the string and so making the pitch of the note waver up and down.

VOLUME CONTROL

▶ Turning this knob up and down to vary the volume of the guitar is often used only to increase volume before a solo and decrease it afterward. Experiment with manipulating the volume control during a solo to appreciate the range of effects. In the very effective but little used technique known as violining, the volume is increased while a note is being played. It works well used over a down bend (see page 104).

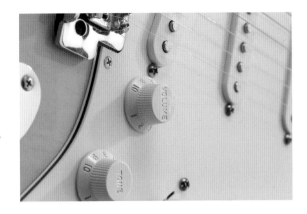

◀ **Violining exercise 1**
Play a note on the D string, turn the volume down and pre-bend the string upward ready to execute a down bend. As you strike the note and slowly release the string to its normal pitch, fade the volume control with the finger of your right hand.

◀ **Violining exercise 2**
Play a note and very quickly continually wind the volume on and off. It is usually best to do this with the little finger of your right hand so the volume control moves up and down as you move your hand.

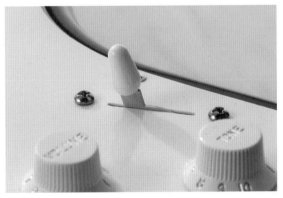

▲ **Tone control**
Playing with the tone dial during a solo can change how much attack a note has. Winding it up increases treble and winding it down increases bass. Repeat the two exercises above using this control.

▲ **Pick-up selector**
By adjusting which pick-up is working you can change the sound of a note. Make yourself familiar with the different settings on your instrument, then experiment by moving the selector around during a solo to give a range of different sounds.

SWEEP picking

The word sweep is used to describe the action of the right hand in this technique, which sweeps gently down and up with no double picks on any strings. The technique, popularized by many rock players, originated as a jazz riff known as gliss (or glissando) picking for its very fast, smooth sound. Using hammer-ons and pull-offs is essential to create the right effect (see page 105). To be able to sweep fluently you must also work on mastering wrist action: it should pivot smoothly, allowing you to sweep down, then up without hesitation. The following exercises will help.

TOP TIP

Do not grip the plectrum too tightly; a tight grip makes it harder to move between strings.

EASY WRIST EXERCISES

◄ 1 Play an E chord with your left hand and practise strumming it by sweeping down from the 6th string to the 1st string and then back up from the 1st string to the 6th string. Unlike when playing scales, hit the top string twice: the second note forms the beginning of the second section of the sweep. As you repeat the action count 1 – 2 – 3 – 4 – 5 – 6, accentuating the 1 and 4. This helps you to get the feel for how the sweep should sound used over more complex chords.

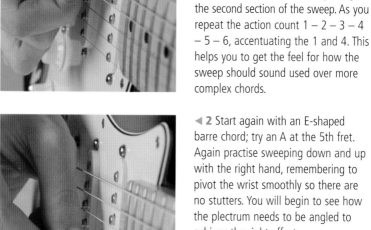

◄ 2 Start again with an E-shaped barre chord; try an A at the 5th fret. Again practise sweeping down and up with the right hand, remembering to pivot the wrist smoothly so there are no stutters. You will begin to see how the plectrum needs to be angled to achieve the right effect.

ADVANCED WRIST EXERCISES

Perfecting the right-handed sweeping motion is only half the technique. To make it sound really good you need to be able to use it over more advanced techniques as the left hand executes hammer-ons and pull-offs.

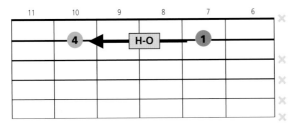

▲ **1** Fret an A-shaped E minor chord, barring the 7th fret with your first finger. Pick the A string with a down stroke of the plectrum and hammer the fourth finger of the left hand on to the 10th fret.

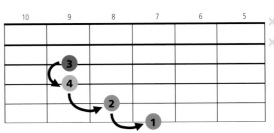

▲ **2** Quickly put your little finger back in place on the 9th fret on the G string and sweep downward with the plectrum until you reach the 1st string.

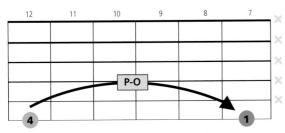

▲ **3** Then place the little finger on the 12th fret of the 1st string and pick upward with the plectrum, immediately pulling the little finger off to release the first finger on the 7th fret.

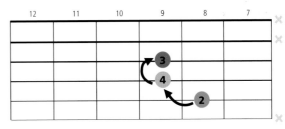

▲ **4** Again, quickly put the little finger back in place on the 9th fret of the G string and sweep upward with the plectrum until you reach the 4th string.

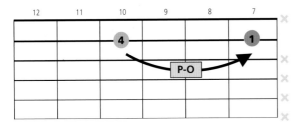

▲ **5** Now place your fourth finger on the 10th fret of the A string, play it with an up stroke of the plectrum and quickly pull off to release the first finger on the 7th fret.

LESSON SUMMARY

By working through this chapter and returning to the work on scales and modes in Lesson 6 (see pages 82–101) your individual soloing style should be improving and your confidence in improvising building. The trick is to start slowly and grow gradually. Now you have got this far, keep working at scales and modes – the best tools there are for becoming a good soloist and improviser.

LESSON 8 UNDERSTANDING TABLATURE

AIM TO BE ABLE TO UNDERSTAND AND READ THE TYPES OF TABLATURE COMMONLY USED ON THE INTERNET AND IN MUSIC BOOKS.

Tablature is divided into bars, in the same way as music on a staff, and the notes are written in place in the bars to give some indication of the timing of the piece. Normally tab gives no indication as to which fingers you should use, but in this lesson you will find the colour-coding we have used throughout the book.

Reading TABLATURE

A tablature, or tab chart, is made up of six horizontal lines, each of which represents one string on the guitar. The top line is the low E string (6th) and the bottom line is the high E string (1st). Numbers written on these lines show which fret is to be played, for example O represents an open string and 4 indicates that the 4th fret should be played.

TABLATURE LEGEND

Many different markings are used in tablature to represent techniques and they can be quite complex, and so sometimes difficult to grasp. Play through all the techniques set out on these pages. Some will be familiar, others may not, but work through each carefully and don't move on until you have a clear understanding of each one.

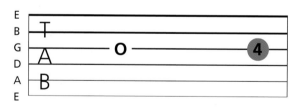

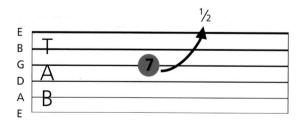

▲ **Semitone bend**
Bend the note up one semitone after playing it.

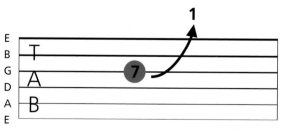

▲ **Whole tone bend**
Bend the note up a whole tone after playing it.

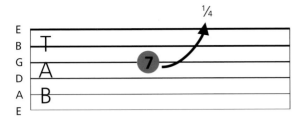

▲ Slight bend, or microtone bend
Bend the note up a quarter tone after playing it.

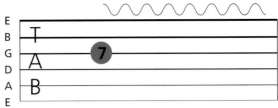

▲ Vibrato
Use one of the three types of vibrato studied in Lesson 7 (see page 106) to create this effect.

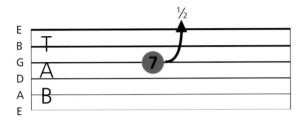

▲ Grace note bend
Bend the note up immediately after playing it. The degree of bend is determined by the number next to the fret mark.

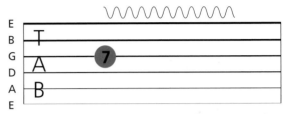

▲ Heavy vibrato, or wide vibrato
Create greater variation in the pitch of the note with a more vigorous action by the left hand.

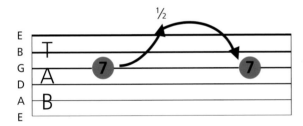

▲ Up and down bend, or bend and release
Bend the note up as far as indicated and release the bend back to the pitch you started at. Pick only the first note with the right hand.

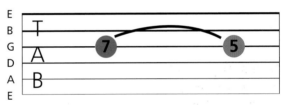

▲ Pull-off
Fret both notes to be sounded, play the higher of the two notes, then immediately pull this finger off to release the lower of the two notes. The change in pitch should be from high to low.

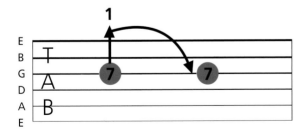

▲ Down bend
Sometimes referred to as a 'pre-bend'. Bend the note before picking it with the right hand, then release the bend back to the starting point.

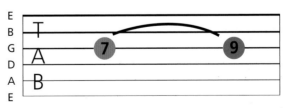

▲ Hammer-on
Fret both notes to be sounded, play the lower of two notes, then immediately hammer the second note on: the change in pitch will be from low to high.

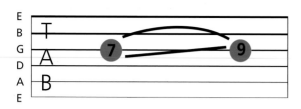

▲ Slide, or *legato* slide
Play the first note and smoothly slide your finger either up or down to the second note.

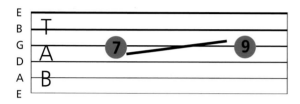

▲ Shift slide
Keep the left-hand action as for an ordinary slide, but also pick the second note with the right hand.

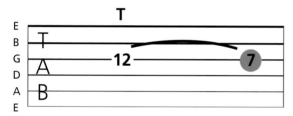

▲ Tapping
Tap the fret marked with a T with the middle finger of the right hand and pull it off to the lower note marked on the tab.

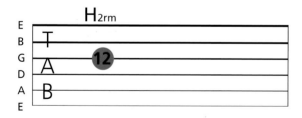

▲ Harmonic
Play the note while the left hand gently touches the string over the fret wire indicated.

P. H.

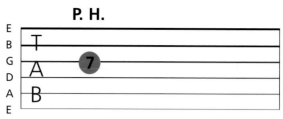

▲ Pinch harmonic
Fret the note normally and produce the harmonic by catching the string with your thumb as you pick it with your plectrum.

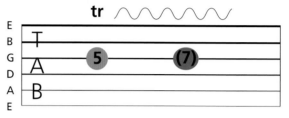

▲ Trill
Rapidly alternate between the two indicated notes, using hammer-ons and pull-offs.

P. M.

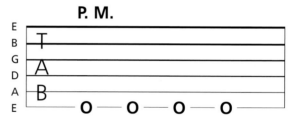

▲ Palm muting
Allow the palm of your right hand softly to mute the sound by resting gently against the strings just before the bridge.

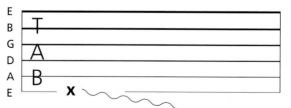

▲ Pick scrape
Use the edge of the plectrum to scrape down or up the strings, which produces a scratchy noise. Sounds particularly effective when using overdrive (see page 131).

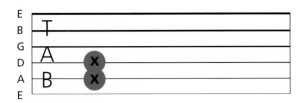

▲ Dampened or muffled strings

Dampen the notes by laying your finger on the strings without pressing them against the fingerboard.

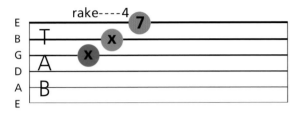

▲ Rake

Similar to sweep picking in that you rake downward with the plectrum over the strings indicated.

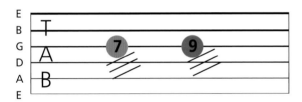

▲ Tremolo picking

Pick the note indicated as rapidly and continuously as possible with your plectrum.

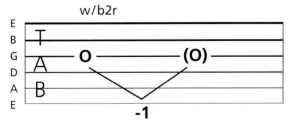

▲ Tremolo arm, or vibrato bar, dive and return

Drop the pitch of the note indicated by the specified amount using the tremolo arm, then return to its original pitch. This is usually done in the same rhythm as the piece of music being played.

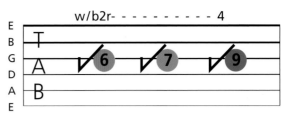

▲ Tremolo arm, or vibrato bar, scoop

Before playing each indicated note, depress the tremolo arm slightly and then quickly release it, creating a rising effect.

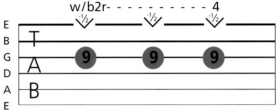

▲ Tremolo arm, or vibrato bar, dip

After playing the note immediately drop its pitch by the specified number of steps using the tremolo arm. Always release back to the original pitch.

JARGON BUSTER

Legato Italian term meaning to play in a smooth, even style without a break between two notes.

LESSON SUMMARY

After digesting this terminology and trying out the techniques, you should be able to read and play along with tab in book form and downloaded from the Internet.

LESSON 9 ARPEGGIOS AND CHORD EXTENSIONS

AIM TO UNDERSTAND HOW ARPEGGIOS ARE FORMED AND HOW THEY ARE THE BASIS OF ALL CHORD SHAPES. ALSO, HOW ARPEGGIOS CAN BE EXTENDED TO CREATE INTERESTING SOUNDS.

An arpeggio is played by picking out the notes that make up a chord in order. Understanding how to build arpeggios is essential as a guitarist, since it forms the basis of all chord building and chord extension theory and helps you to name unknown chords.

ARPEGGIOS

In Lesson 4 you learnt eight basic arpeggios, starting with the major arpeggio, looked at some basic one-octave variants, and worked up to the major 7th arpeggio (see pages 63–64). In this lesson we move into a second octave. We also study how a chord name tells us everything we need to know in order to be able to play that chord.

BASIC ARPEGGIO FORMULA

A basic formula can be applied to most arpeggios: 1st – 3rd – 5th – 7th – 9th – 11th – 13th. It tells us that all these notes in the scale are important in the general make up of a chord and so an arpeggio must contain them. Building an arpeggio is rather like building a wall; if you remove one of the notes the arpeggio doesn't work, in the same way that if you remove a course of bricks, the wall falls down. Deciding which variations of each note we need for each individual chord is the tricky bit, but chord names always give a fair indication of what is required.

Looking at arpeggios

Look at the make up of a minor 9th arpeggio: it contains the 1st – ♭3rd – 5th – ♭7th – 9th notes of a scale. Compare it with the construction of a major 9th arpeggio: 1st – 3rd – 5th – 7th – 9th. The two subtle differences at the 3rd and 7th notes make a huge difference to the sound of the chord or arpeggio.

Now look at a dominant 9th arpeggio to see how this is built: 1st – 3rd – 5th – ♭7th – 9th. Again it looks and sounds slightly different from the two preceding patterns. Notice that the 9th note remains unchanged in all three arpeggios. It is a common misconception to presume the m9th arpeggio takes the ♭9th (or minor 9th) note: the ♭9th is only used when the chord name mentions it, for example in Am7♭9.

9TH ARPEGGIOS

We will study 9th arpeggios by learning all the arpeggios in the key of A.
Remember that they can be transposed anywhere on the fingerboard. Progress
through them one by one.

▶ **A9th note pattern:**
1, 3, 5, ♭7, 9
Try this out on the fingerboard
and notice how the ♭7th is
used because it is dominant.

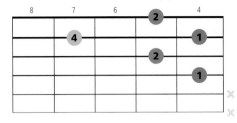

▶ **Amaj9th note pattern:**
1, 3, 5, 7, 9
When playing, think about
how this arpeggio uses a
major 3rd and a major 7th;
this is because the chord name
states 'major' in its title.

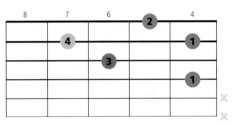

▶ **Am9th note pattern:**
1, ♭3, 5, ♭7, 9
Play through, noting how the
♭7th note is used in this
arpeggio but this time with the
♭3rd note.

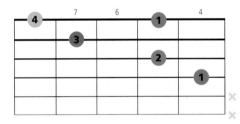

11TH ARPEGGIOS

Here we begin to see how the basis of the arpeggios remains the same but a new
note is added to the end each time. This pattern continues when we go on to
study 13th arpeggios.

▶ **A11th note pattern:**
1, 3, 5, ♭7, 9, 11
When playing through notice
again how the ♭7th is used in
this arpeggio.

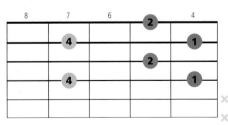

▶ **Amaj11th note pattern:**
1, 3, 5, 7, 9, 11
See how this arpeggio again uses the major 3rd and major 7th notes and continues up to an 11th note.

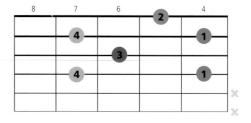

▶ **Am11th note pattern:**
1, ♭3, 5, ♭7, 9, 11
Play through noting the ♭3rd and ♭7th notes again, but this time climbing to an 11th.

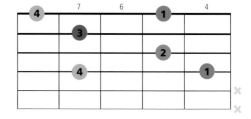

13TH ARPEGGIOS

The pattern continues as you would anticipate: add another note to the end of each arpeggio. Play through each example again, familiarizing yourself with all the finger patterns relating to these arpeggios.

▶ **A13th note pattern:**
1, 3, 5, ♭7, 9, 11, 13
Play the same notes as in the previous two dominant arpeggios, then add a 13th note at the end.

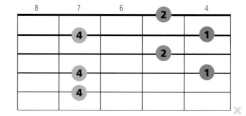

▶ **Amaj13th note pattern:**
1, 3, 5, 7, 9, 11, 13
Repeat the pattern to create this arpeggio.

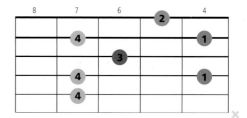

▶ **Am13th note pattern:**
1, ♭3, 5, ♭7, 9, 11, 13
Play through the minor 13th arpeggio following the same pattern as before, adding the final note.

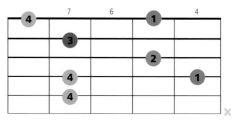

ADJUSTED CHORD ARPEGGIOS

All the arpeggios we have studied so far use very straightforward patterns; there is no sharpening or flattening of notes within the chord names. This makes them relatively easy to work out. When an adjusted note forms part of a chord name, it requires careful thinking about how to build the arpeggio. For example, if the chord name states that the 5th note is ♭5th, you must flatten the 5th note.

▶ **Am7♭5 note pattern:**
1, ♭3, ♭5, ♭7
Play through, noticing how the 3rd, 5th and 7th notes are all flattened.

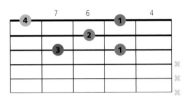

▶ **A7♭5#9 note pattern:**
1, 3, ♭5, ♭7, #9
Play through, thinking about how the 7th has to be dominant because the chord name doesn't state major or minor.

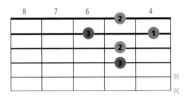

▶ **Amaj7#5 note pattern:**
1, 3, #5, 7
Work through on the fingerboard to see how the 5th note has been sharpened to F from E.

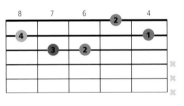

▶ **Am7♭5♭9 note pattern:**
1, ♭3, ♭5, ♭7, ♭9
When you are practising, note that the 3rd note has to be minor and the 7th has to be dominant.

▶ **A7#9 note pattern:**
1, 3, 5, ♭7, #9
When playing, note that the 3rd is major, that the 7th is dominant and that the 9th is sharpened by a semitone.

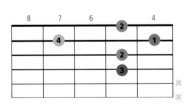

▶ **Amaj7#5#9 note pattern:**
1, 3, #5, 7, #9
The 7th is major this time, this is only because the name of the chord clearly has major in it.

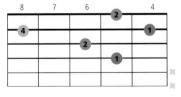

Chord EXTENSIONS

What are these? Chords with notes added to change the sound. Musicians usually add a 9th, 11th or 13th note to a chord, but notes can be sharpened or flattened, too, to produce even more options. Guitarists can't play all the notes in an arpeggio when fretting a chord extension; we must carefully choose the most important notes and find fingerings that are easy to fret so we can incorporate these new chord shapes into our playing regularly. Many musicians include more than one version of a note in a chord; what's important is that the main notes feature so the chord is recognizable as an extension.

TOP TIP

The maximum number of notes that can be played simultaneously on a guitar is six – there are only six strings. The more notes, you play the fuller the chord will sound. You might sometimes need to lie a finger across more than one string at a time to achieve the chord shape: feel free to use any finger, not just the first.

THREE MAIN TYPES

As with arpeggios, there are three main types of chord that can be extended: dominant seventh chords, minor seventh chords and major seventh chords. Straight major or minor chords can't be extended because the arpeggio finishes on the octave note, closing the door to the second octave. When we play one of the three seventh chords, the arpeggio stops on the 7th note, leaving the door open for us to move into the second octave. Sixth chords are a kind of reverse chord extension because although they don't run as high as the 7th note, they are based on the three chords we are currently studying.

CHOOSING WHICH NOTES TO USE

The main notes in a chord will always be the 1st, 3rd, 5th and 7th notes of the scale, as these define which type of chord is played. On top of these, the only other important note to play is the extended note mentioned in the chord name.

Easy exercise

1 Create a dominant thirteenth chord by playing the 1st, 3rd, 5th, ♭7th and 13th notes of a scale. As you play the notes, hear the distinct 13th note suggesting exactly which type of thirteenth chord it is, a dominant thirteenth chord.

2 Play the same notes, but flatten the 3rd and hear the difference: now you are playing a minor thirteenth chord.

BASIC CHORD EXTENSION SHAPES

Here are some of the more common extension shapes you will find useful when playing or writing chord charts. Work through them methodically, memorizing the notes and the finger patterns.

◀ D9 note pattern:
1, 3, ♭7, 9, 5

When practising this dominant chord with an added 9th, work closely on lying the third finger flat over three strings.

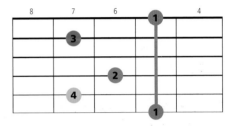

◀ A13 note pattern:
1, 5, ♭7, 10, 13, 8

Play this straight A7 barre chord with the little finger placed on the B string.

◀ Dm9 note pattern:
1, ♭3, ♭7, 9, 5

When playing, notice the similarity in shape to the dominant 9th chord.

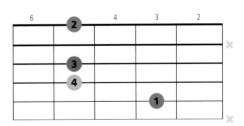

◀ Am11 note pattern:
1, ♭7, ♭10, 11

See how this shape uses the ♭10th to create the minor. Deaden the A string by lying the second finger over it.

◄ Amaj9 note pattern:
1, 3, 7, 9, 5
Persevere with this tricky
chord. Work on fretting the
D string with the fourth finger
while the third finger is on the
B string. Note the part barre
played by the first finger.

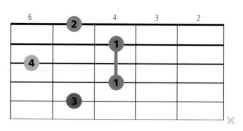

ALTERED CHORDS

An altered chord is a standard chord shape that has one or more notes altered
(sharpened or flattened) to create a new sound. These chords, too, tend to be built
from the three main groups – dominant, minor and major – and usually include
the 7th note.

Easy exercise

Learn the altered chord Am7♭5 by starting with a basic Am7 chord. Play the chord,
then flatten the 5th. To do this, work out which note is the 5th in the scale and
flatten it by a semitone.

BASIC ALTERED CHORD SHAPES

Play around with these shapes on the neck. Some are A string root and some are
E string but they are all transpositional shapes. If you find a particular shape
difficult, keep returning to it until you have mastered it.

◄ Am7♭5 note pattern:
1, ♭7, ♭10, ♭5
When you play through this,
note how similar it is to the
minor 11th chord shape, but
with the 11th note sharpened.
See how the #11th is the
same as the ♭5th.

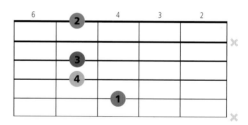

◄ A7#5 note pattern:
1, ♭7, 10, #5
Practise this dominant chord
noting how the 10th note
distinguishes it as major.

◄ D7♭9 note pattern:
1, 3, ♭7, ♭9
Work on lying the first finger down to cover both the D and B strings.

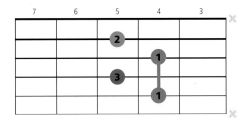

◄ D7#9 note pattern:
1, 3, ♭7, #9
Notice the similarity to D7♭9, adding your little finger to make the difference by creating the #9th note.

TOP TIP

Play around with chord shapes: moving notes around within a chord often produces a better sound. A♭5th at the bottom of a chord can sound quite muddy, for instance: move it up an octave and hear how enhanced the sound is.

LESSON SUMMARY

You have worked logically through basic arpeggio patterns, arpeggios with added 9th, 11th and 13th notes, and less straightforward adjusted chord patterns. You will find this work not only very useful for building chords, but also a great tool when soloing. Understanding how to build arpeggios has given you the knowledge to be able to extend chords widely. You have practised chord extensions patiently on the fingerboard and have also mastered altered chord shapes, which you will encounter regularly in most styles of music.

LESSON 10 MUSICAL STYLES AND MOVING ON

AIM TO BE ABLE TO APPRECIATE A WIDE RANGE OF MUSICAL STYLES AND UNDERSTAND THE DIFFERENCES BETWEEN VARIOUS TYPES OF EQUIPMENT AND HOW THEY ARE USED.

Congratulations. You have reached the final lesson in the book. Working through the previous lessons will have equipped you to play successfully within many musical styles. You should now try to develop a wide-ranging appreciation of different types of music.

Musical STYLES

We tend to gravitate toward styles of music that touch us, listening to particular artists and songs that feel comfortable. This is great, but a good musician doesn't let favourite sounds close his or her ears to other types of music. Many guitarists get hooked on one famous player because of their image or the type of guitar they play. Try not to be this short sighted: you can only benefit from exploring guitarists from all musical genres.

TOP TIP

Don't get hung up on being cool. Listen to what you want, and if you don't think your friends will think you're cool, don't tell them.

BE ADVENTUROUS

Many guitarists, and rock musicians generally, openly state that they dislike classical music, because it is 'boring', or write off jazz as discordant. Make it part of your musical education to try a little Bach and Mozart, John Coltrane, Miles Davis and Pat Metheny. Listen not just for the tunes, but the rhythmic patterns and the use of dynamics. Spot in their work striking chord changes and use of modes. Notice instruments playing in an ensemble and follow soloists as they weave over other players. Pick out a theme and see how many variations the composer or improviser conjures up.

Listen to guitarists working in styles as diverse as tango, dub and new wave. Move beyond guitarists and listen to anything and everything you can get your hands on: Balinese Gamelan, Italian opera, Appalachian folk songs. One of them might turn your life around, change your playing immeasurably for the better or set you on a musical path you'd never previously considered. Listen, even, to music you actively dislike, whether it's free jazz or modern electronica. However strange, everything feeds into your musical repertoire. Get lost in new musical worlds and the horizons of your own playing will expand.

Listening exercise

1 Every month buy yourself an album or download tracks by a musician, group or composer you've never listened to before. Take the advice of friends or fellow musicians, if you wish, but make sure the artist is new to you.

2 Listen to the recording all the way through. If it's on vinyl, turn over and play the other side. Whether you like it or not, make yourself listen to it at least five times. Watch how your opinion evolves.

3 If you like, or even just appreciate, the recording, explore the artist's previously recorded work.

4 Write down the names of other musicians who played on the tracks and follow them up (this works especially well in jazz). Who produced the sound? Is the recording on a label that specializes in a particular type of music? Look for more recordings from the same labels.

5 Every year look back at what has remained with you, what you jettisoned and how your tastes have broadened over that period.

EFFECTS and EQUIPMENT

You can choose to enhance the tone of your guitar with a host of products. Amplifiers come fully loaded with effects and gadgets these days, and a massive number of effects units are available to give all manner of different sounds.

WHAT IS AN EFFECTS UNIT?

An effects unit plugs into an amplifier at one end and your guitar at the other. Often they come in the form of pedals, which you stand on to turn on and off to alter the sound of the guitar massively (for a description of some of the effects, see right). Hundreds of different types of effects can be used, all offering something slightly different. Many guitarists like the tone of pedals, but you must consider the expense of buying more than one.

Multi-effects units contain a range of effects, cutting out the need for a row of pedals on the floor by your feet when you play. The obvious advantages of this system are the compact size and the cost (about the equivalent of two pedals), but some musicians dislike the 'digital', or slightly sterile, tone.

▲ Effects pedals come in all different shapes and sizes and provide a wide array of sounds.

▲ Multi-effects pedals are a cost-effective way of having many different effects in one box.

▲ Wah-wah pedals are very funky and sound great in all styles of music.

Effects to try

Overdrive Adds a warm crunch to the sound of your guitar.

Distortion A more severe form of overdrive, producing a rich screaming tone.

Wah-wah Worked with the foot as the pedal is on a pivot which is pressed and depressed to produce a 'wah-wah' tone.

Chorus Gently modulates the pitch and depth of a note.

Phaser Produces an effect similar to a rotating speaker.

Flanger A mix of phaser and chorus that gives a rather space-age sounding effect.

Digital delay Acts like an echo, so used to create the effect of more than one guitar playing.

Reverb Found on most amplifiers and adds a shimmering echo effect to the sound of the guitar.

TOP TIP

Practice amplifiers are designed for home use and are generally around 10 or 15 watts – quiet enough to use in a bedroom. They often come equipped with reverb and distortion. An amplifier loud enough for public performance needs to be around 80–100 watts.

AMPLIFIERS

A good deal of jargon attaches to amplifiers and the subject can be confusing. Familiarize yourself with the following terms to cut through the confusion.

Watts The degree by which the volume of the amplifier is measured. The higher the watts, the louder the amplifier.

Bass, middle, treble Equalization controls used to change the sound of your guitar through the amplifier.

Gain Another word for overdrive (see left). Drives the pre-amplifier hard to make it sound fuzzy.

Pre-amp The section of the amplifier where the sound of the guitar is taken in, before being sent out of the speakers.

Cabs Abbreviation of 'cabinet', which refers to a speaker cabinet. These can be stacked on top of one another to form walls of sound. They always require an amplifier to work.

Head Short for amplifier head. Plug your guitar into one of these and then connect the head to a speaker cab.

Twin channel Two different channels, one for clean sound and one for overdrive.

General MAINTENANCE

Looking after your guitar is essential if you want it to perform always at its best. It is astounding how many guitarists let the strings on their guitar die so that they sound muffled and dull, and then just replace an odd string when one breaks. Five dull strings and one bright new string makes for a ludicrous sound.

EVERYDAY CARE

Always wipe your guitar after playing: perspiration can cause a tarnishing of the lacquered surface. Don't forget to wipe the back of the neck, where sticky thumb marks can build up, resulting in slower movement of the thumb when playing.

How to clean your guitar

Try to get into the habit of restringing your guitar before a string breaks. This way you can remove all the old strings, clean your guitar thoroughly and then restring it knowing the new strings will last longer because the fingerboard is clean.

1 Remove all the strings from your guitar.

2 Clean the fret wires using fine wire wool or a brass cleaning product. Wipe away any residue immediately to prevent staining.

3 If your guitar has a rosewood or dark wood fingerboard, apply a wood oil, such as lemon oil or linseed oil, to lubricate the frets. Let the oil soak in before wiping the residue away with a dry lint-free cloth.

4 Now the neck is clean it is ready to be restrung (see page 15).

TOP TIPS

- Do not run a duster underneath your strings to clean the body or fingerboard of your guitar. Tiny pieces of fabric will wrap around the strings: not only do they make the strings sound dull and muted, they are impossible to remove.

- Never leave your guitar next to a radiator or in a car for a prolonged period and never store your guitar in an attic. Extreme temperature can seriously damage your guitar because it is made of wood, and wood bends and moves when it gets too hot or cold.

Preventing messy leads

1 When you unplug a lead, fold it in half so that you hold the two *jack plugs* in one hand and the folded end of the lead in the other. If the lead is long enough, you can fold it in half again.

2 Holding the two ends of the folded lead with both hands, tie the lead into a neat knot.

3 Place the lead into your bag or case without getting it tangled, ready to untie next time you want to use it.

JARGON BUSTER

Jack plugs The two ends of a lead that plug into your electric guitar at one end and into the amplifier at the other.

LESSON SUMMARY

In this final lesson you have started to challenge your preconceptions about which types of music you like, because openmindedness is the key to becoming a great guitarist and a great musician. You have become familiar with a range of effects and the components of an amplifier, and discovered how to look after your guitar to keep it in good working order and to ensure it plays well.

CHORD DIRECTORY

This resource offers 382 of the most useful chords a guitarist needs. Because every chord can be played in many different ways and using various finger positions, beginners can find them rather confusing. The pages that follow provide the answer: one shape for each of the most commonly used chords written in every key, enabling you to find the chord you are looking for quickly and easily. So, when you are learning a new song and you need to play chords you have never seen before, don't panic! Find the chord in this directory and you can successfully complete the song.

A chords

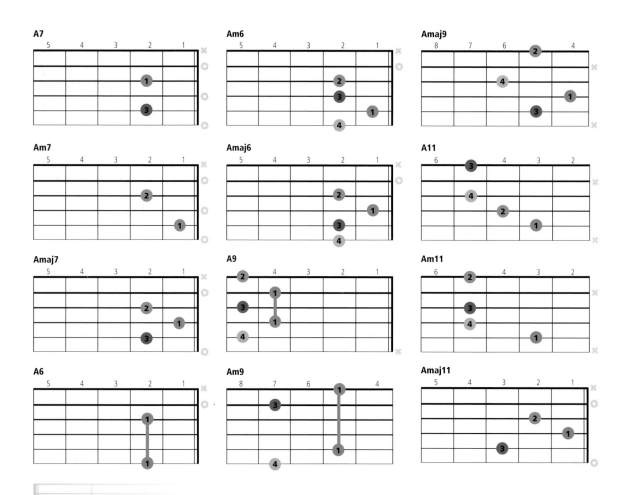

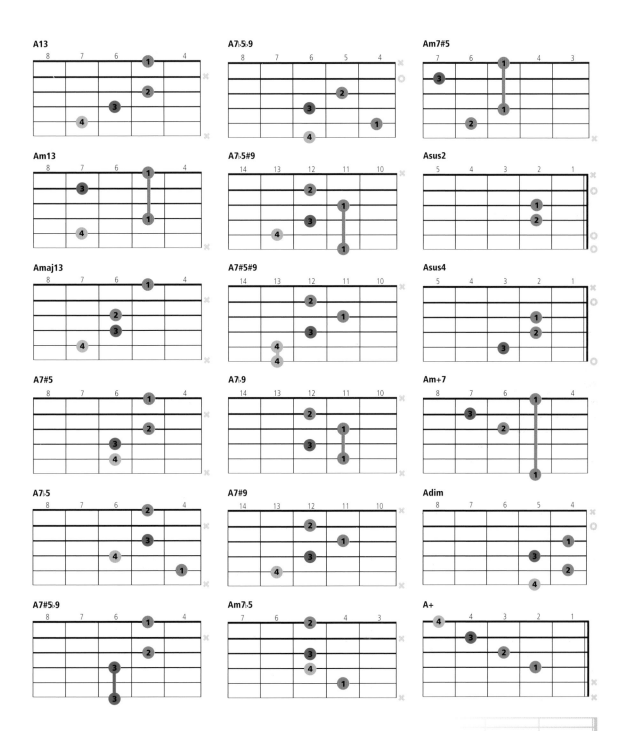

A# / B♭ chords

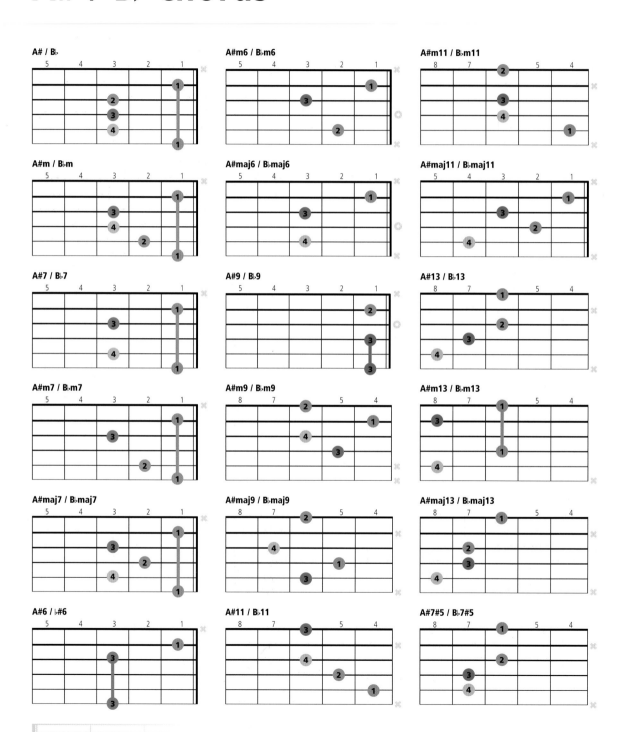

A# / B♭

A#m6 / B♭m6

A#m11 / B♭m11

A#m / B♭m

A#maj6 / B♭maj6

A#maj11 / B♭maj11

A#7 / B♭7

A#9 / B♭9

A#13 / B♭13

A#m7 / B♭m7

A#m9 / B♭m9

A#m13 / B♭m13

A#maj7 / B♭maj7

A#maj9 / B♭maj9

A#maj13 / B♭maj13

A#6 / ♭#6

A#11 / B♭11

A#7#5 / B♭7#5

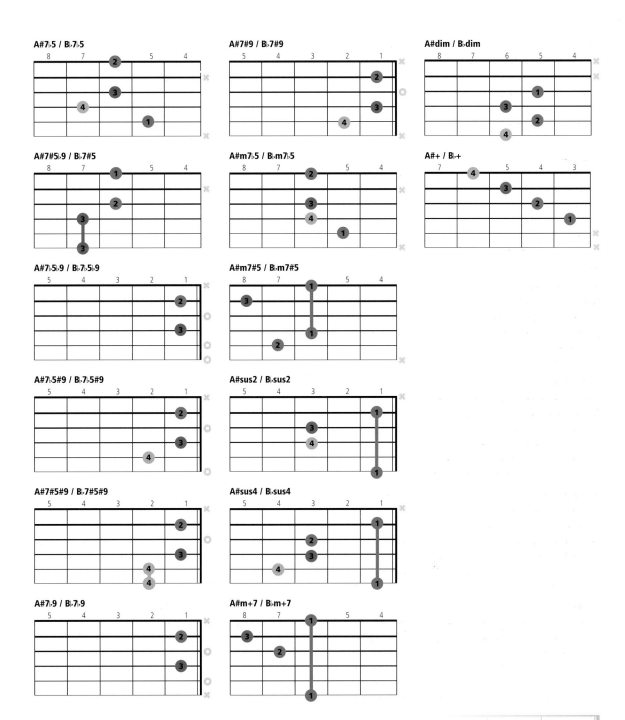

B chords

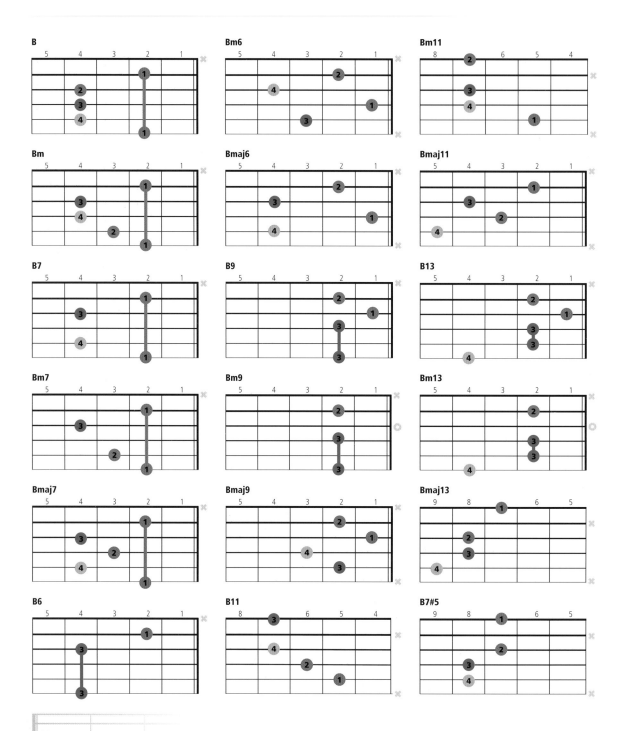

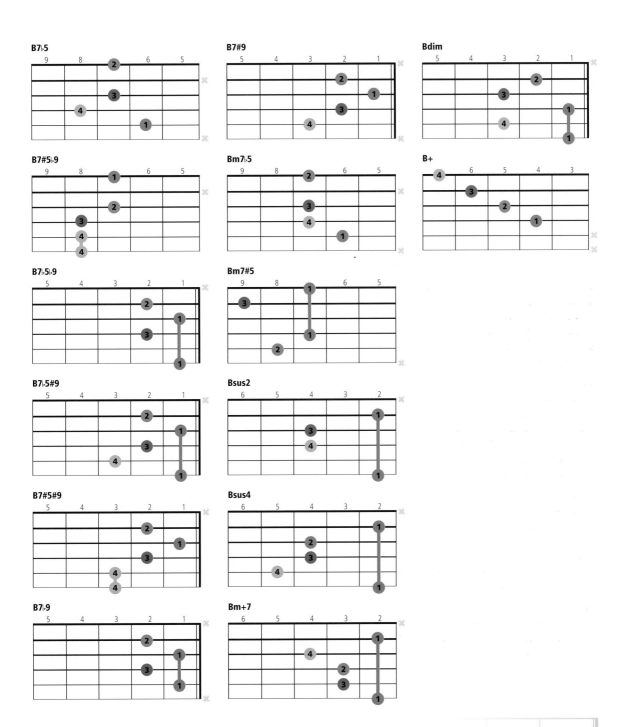

C chords

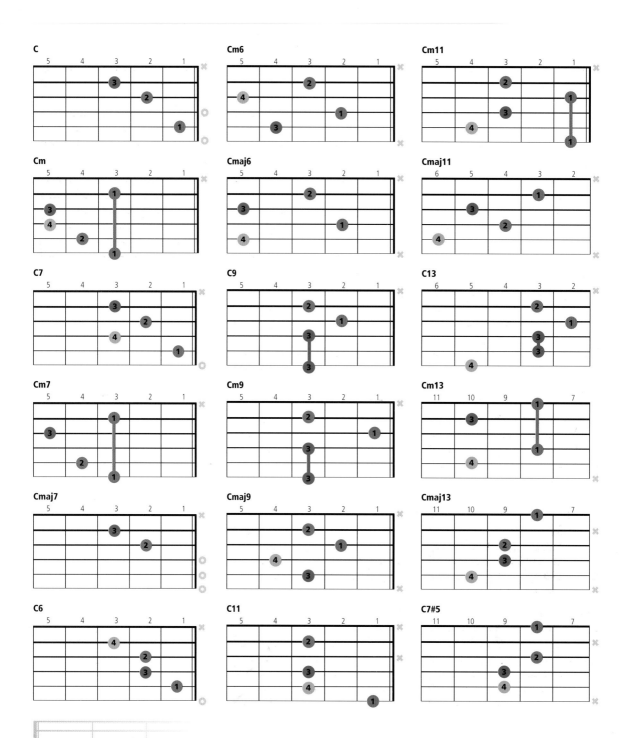

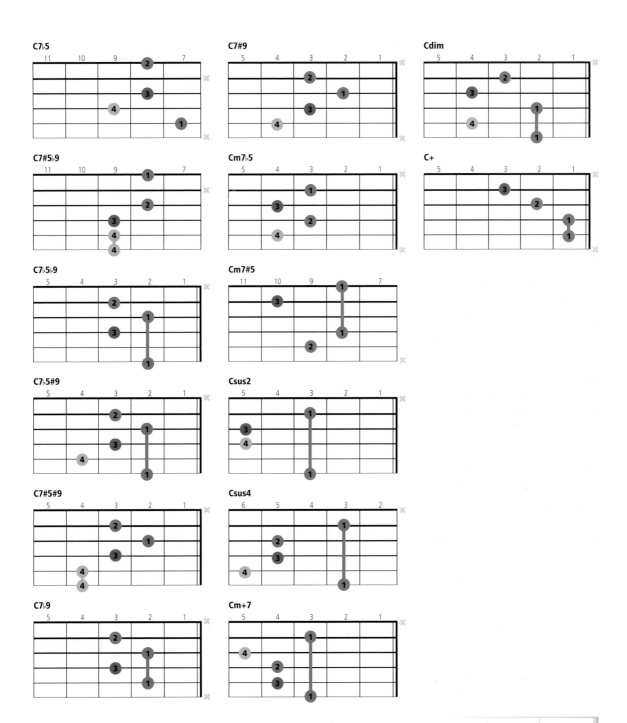

C# / D♭ chords

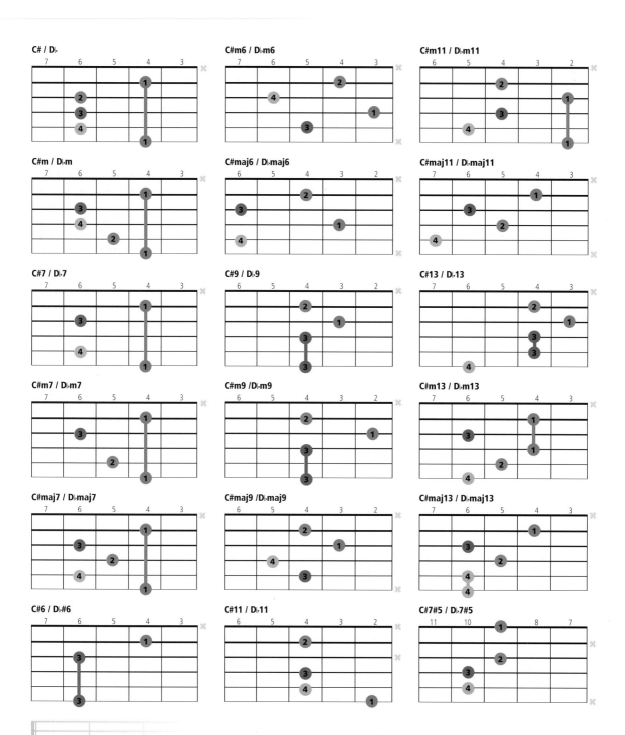

C# / D♭

C#m6 / D♭m6

C#m11 / D♭m11

C#m / D♭m

C#maj6 / D♭maj6

C#maj11 / D♭maj11

C#7 / D♭7

C#9 / D♭9

C#13 / D♭13

C#m7 / D♭m7

C#m9 / D♭m9

C#m13 / D♭m13

C#maj7 / D♭maj7

C#maj9 / D♭maj9

C#maj13 / D♭maj13

C#6 / D♭#6

C#11 / D♭11

C#7#5 / D♭7#5

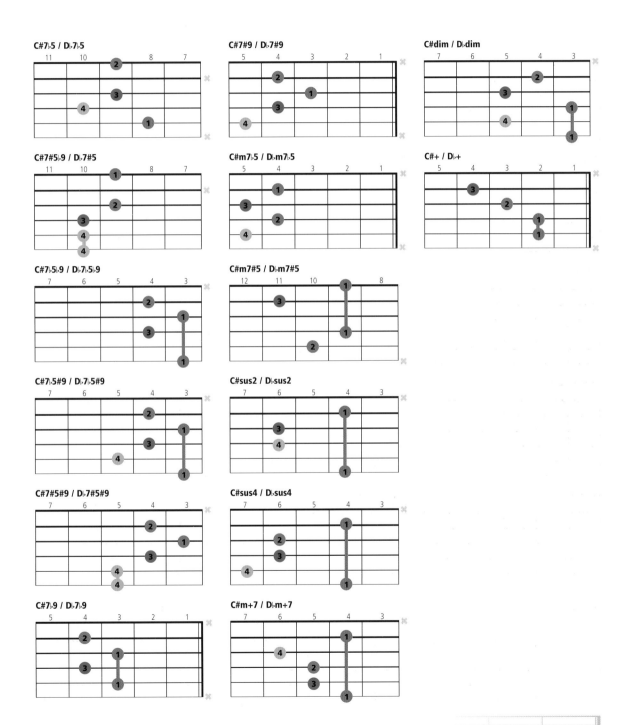

D chords

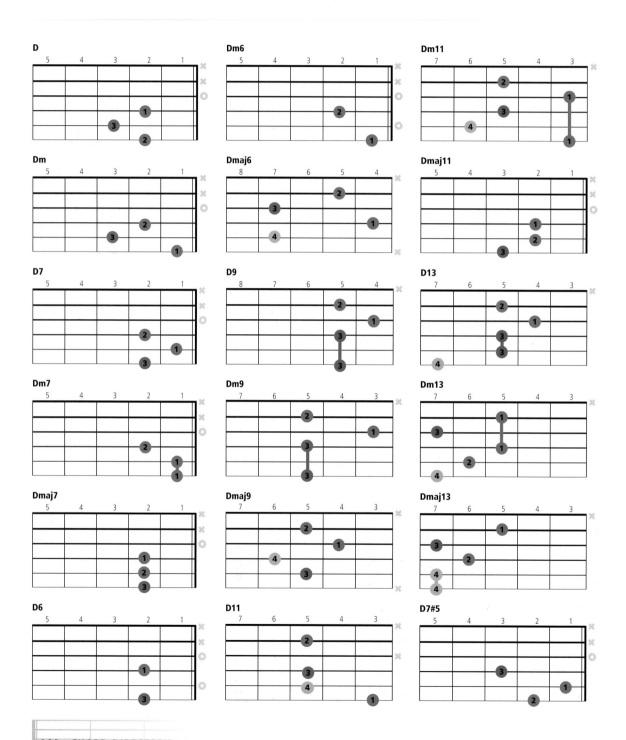

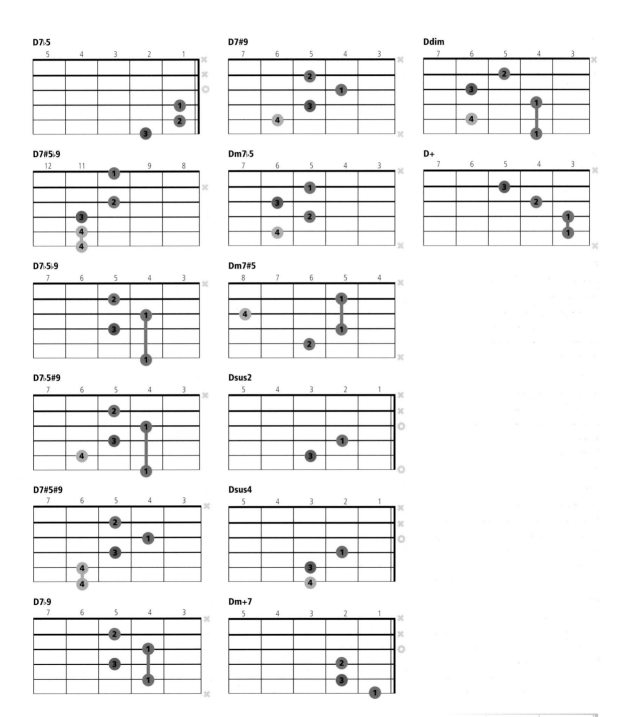

D# / E♭ chords

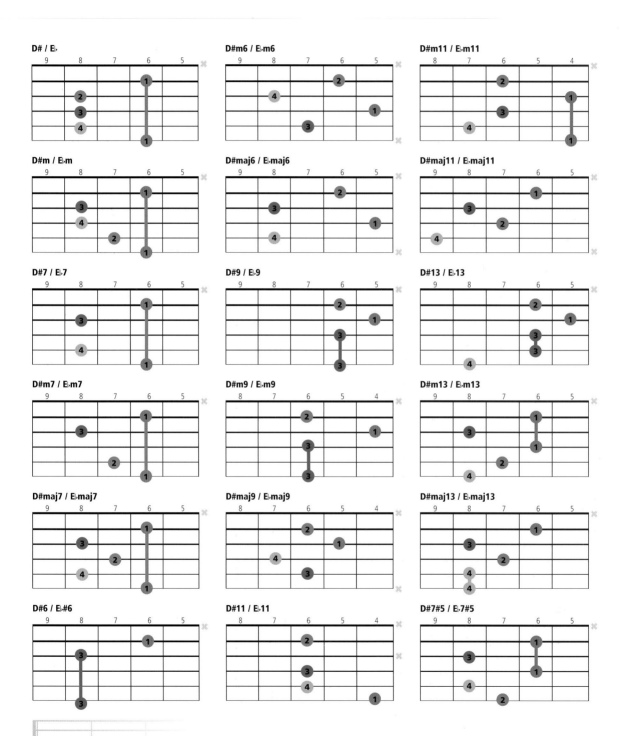

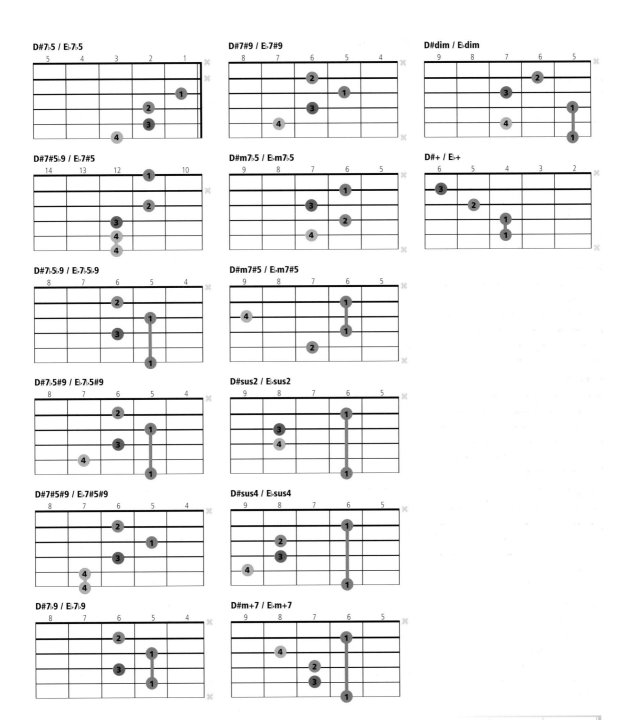

E chords

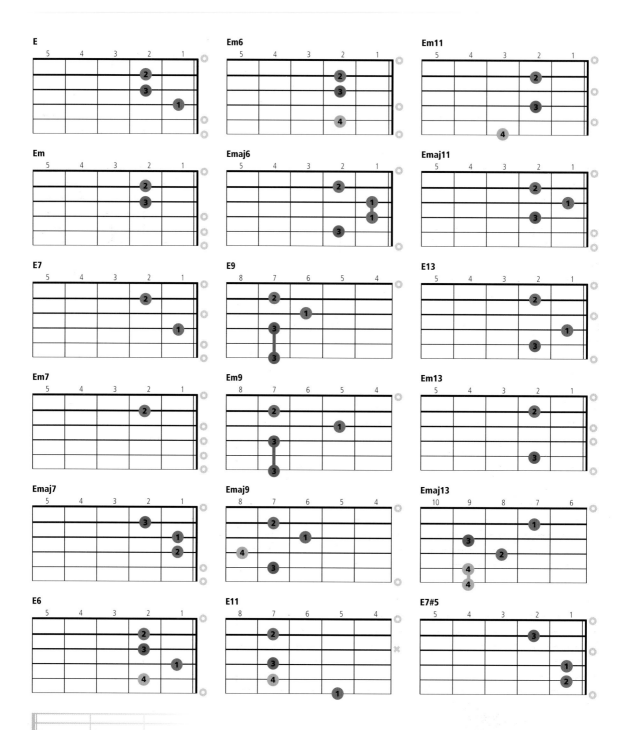

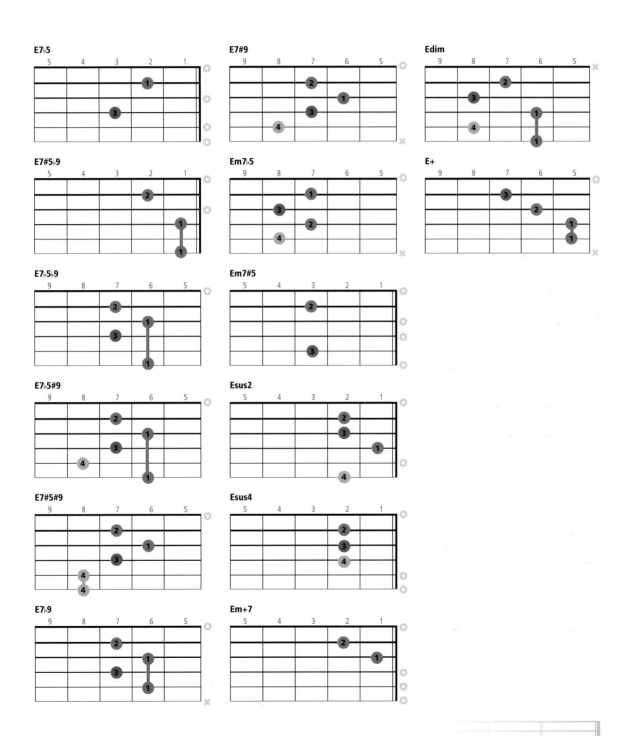

F chords

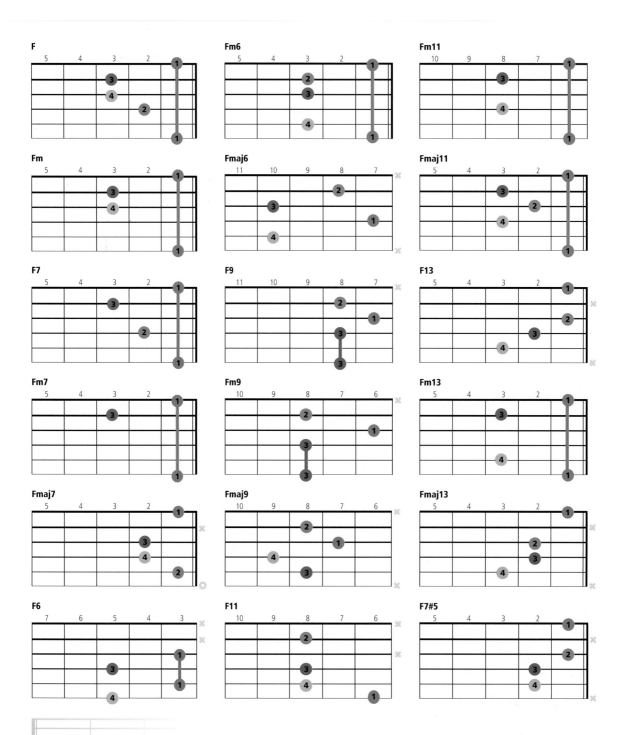

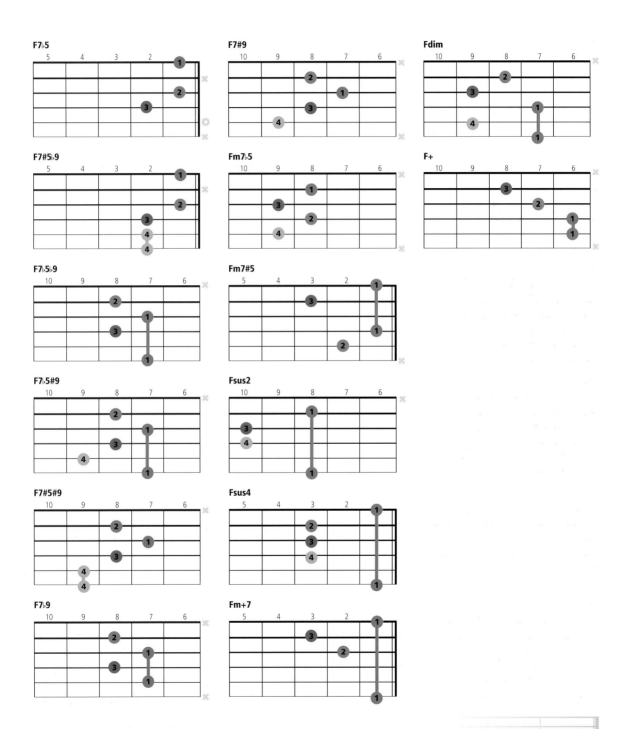

F# / G♭ chords

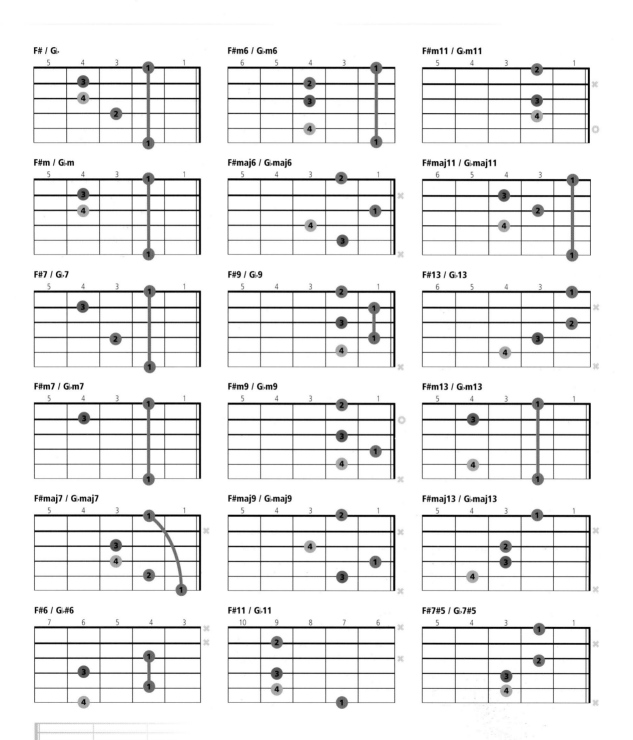

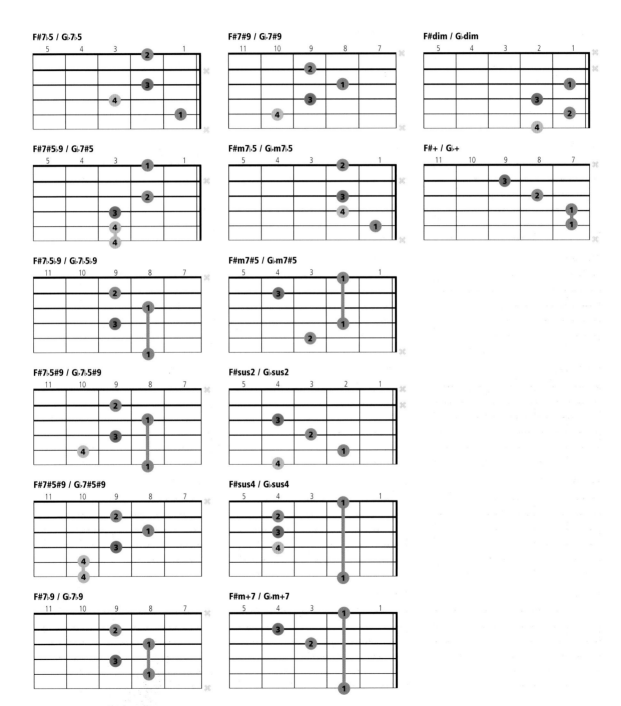

G chords

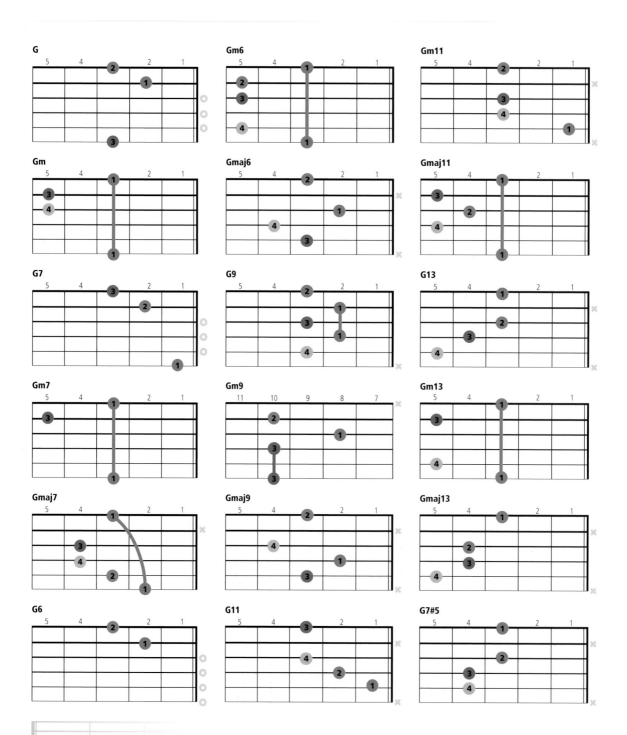

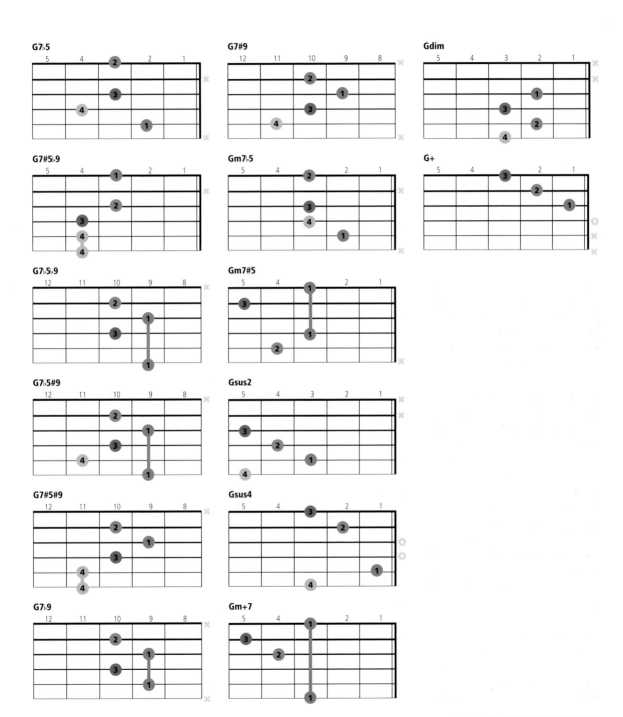

G# / A♭ chords

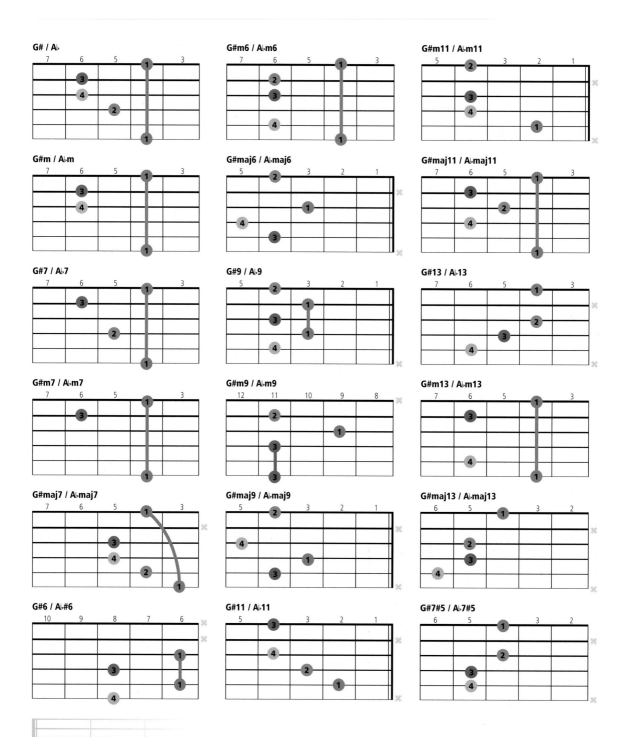

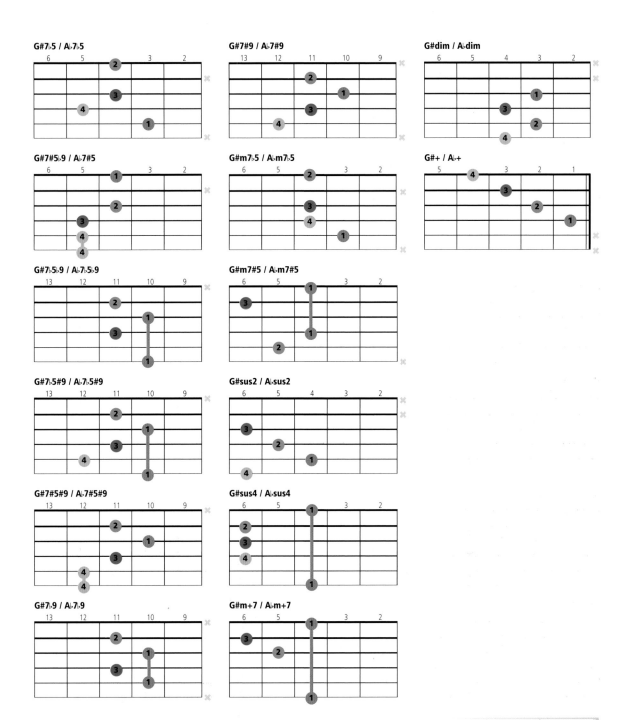

INDEX

ACKNOWLEDGEMENTS

Executive Editor Trevor Davies
Project Editor Leanne Bryan
Executive Art Editor Darren Southern
Designer Darren Bland, Cobalt id
Photographer Mike Prior
Senior Production Controller Martin Croshaw
Picture Researcher Jennifer Veall

Special photography © Octopus Publishing Group
Limited/Mike Prior.

Thanks to our wonderful models, Jon Buck, Ivor Sims and
Fujie Yoshimoto, and to the team at Sound Control, Oxford
Street, for their kind loan of equipment.

Jon Buck is a multi-instrumentalist whose first instrument
of choice is guitar. He runs a guitar/bass tuition business and
is a member of the Registry of Guitar Tutors. Jon plays and
teaches all styles of music and has worked with artists as
diverse as Hank Roberts and Tino Gonzales. To get more
information and find out about CD releases, log on to
www.jonbuck.co.uk

BCPL
Baltimore County
Public Library